Dancing
Through Life

Dancing
Through Life

CANDACE CAMERON BURE

PUBLISHING GROUP
NASHVILLE, TENNESSEE

Published by B&H Publishing Group
Nashville, Tennessee

Dewey Decimal Classification: 248.84
Subject Heading: CHRISTIAN LIFE \ COURAGE \
BURE, CANDACE CAMERON

1 2 3 4 5 6 7 8 • 20 19 18 17 16 15

Dedication

To my dear husband and sweet children:
Without your courage, patience, support,
and enthusiasm none of this would have been possible.
Thank you for your willingness to step out of your comfort
zone by allowing me to step out of mine. I dedicate this
book to you, for you are my everything. I love you.

Acknowledgments

Mark Ballas—I couldn't imagine taking this pilgrimage with anyone else. You not only taught me how to dance but taught me so much about myself in the process. I don't know how to express in words the depths of what you and this journey have meant to me. It changed me. Forever. You are an incredibly talented man who has patience beyond measure and your goofiness is golden. I will always be cheering you on your life's journey and am blessed to call you my friend. Love you—forever your Edna Flemington.

Erin Davis—I wasn't sure if I could write this with someone who doesn't own a television, but you proved yourself a rock star! (Not that I didn't already know.) I am incredibly grateful for your wisdom, knowledge, guidance, and artful skill of writing.

D.J. Candyball Prayer Team—I was able to dance this journey because of each and every prayer you sent up for me. The warmth and comfort of knowing I was being covered in God's grace through your words allowed me to take each step forward no matter how difficult it was at the moment. I will always be praying for each of you.

Jennifer Lyell, Jana Spooner, Melissa Fuller, and the B&H Publishing team—Thank you for championing my passion and desire to write about my journey of courage and conviction. Although it was on a whim, the feeling was so strong I knew it was inspired by the Holy Spirit. I'm glad you felt it too.

A HUGE thank you to my rockstar team: Jeffery Brooks and Ford Englerth, Redrock Entertainment, Anderson Group PR, Gersh Agency, Chad Christopher, Tara Brooks, Daniel Blaylock, and Rowan Daly.

A special thank you to Tracy Mapes and Steve Neibert, ABC Television Network, and *Dancing with the Stars.*

To all my lifelong and new fans who supported me through *Dancing with the Stars* and voted for Mark and me every single week by phone and website, THANK YOU!! You're the reason (literally) that I made it to the finish line!

Jesus, sweet Jesus—All praise, glory, and honor is given to You.

Contents

Chapter 1

Ready. Set. Stand!

Let them praise His name with dancing and make
music to Him with tambourine and lyre.
—Psalm 149:3

The cameras were ready. The audience was filled with my family and friends. I was in a costume tailor-made just for me, for this moment. It made me feel beautiful and special. When the music started, I begged my brain to remember the moves I'd been practicing. I begged my body to obey my brain. I forced a smile and started to dance. Once my feet started moving, it didn't take long for joy to bubble up from inside me. The seeds of a dream had been planted. I had no idea that God would plant my feet on a different stage years later and give me the opportunity to turn the spotlight toward Him.

The backdrop of this book is my experience as a contestant on *Dancing with the Stars (DWTS)*. Consider this your all-access pass to the hit show that pairs a celebrity (that's me!) with a professional dancer (so not me!) for ten grueling weeks of dancing competition. Of course, it's much more than that. Even though I love to dance and dreamed of being on the show for nearly a decade, for me, *Dancing with the Stars* became so much more than a dancing competition. It wasn't about being on an Emmy-nominated hit reality competition show or seeing a dream come true while millions watched. I believe that my time on *DWTS* was the opportunity of a lifetime because it allowed me to showcase my faith in Jesus Christ. On a bigger stage than I had ever graced before, I had the chance to be a witness in front of a watching world. Along the journey I learned in many ways what it was like to stand with conviction while being stretched way beyond my comfort zone. I can't wait to share those lessons with you!

That scene of me on a stage in a fabulous dancing costume didn't come from the show. That was me at five years old, the first and only time I remember stepping foot on a stage to dance before I agreed to be on *DWTS*. That moment is a snapshot in my memory from when I took a handful of tap and ballet lessons one summer as a child. My sister Melissa and I took just enough classes to have a single recital at the end of the session.

I don't remember a lot about those lessons except for a vivid flash memory of learning to leap across the ballet floor. While some of the girls were just jumping over an imaginary line with one foot haphazardly in the air, I tried to split my legs and make the move look as graceful as I'd seen real dancers do. In my mind I can hear the teacher say to me, "Yes! Just like that, Candace. Good job!"

Fast-forward more than three decades and this is a picture of my experience on *DWTS*. I didn't just want to be on a show. I didn't just want to learn to dance. I knew what my invisible lines were. I knew where I would not cross. Those lines were my convictions, drawn by my time in the Word, the guidance of the Holy Spirit in me, and the accountability offered by my Christian community.

Learning to leap is a great picture of what my experience was like. It was a leap of faith, for sure. But I knew up front that I didn't want to just vault across the *DWTS* stage without a plan. I wanted to move with purpose. I wanted to show what it looked like to live within the boundaries that God gives us for our good and I wanted to do it all while looking graceful to the watching world.

My childhood dancing lessons were short-lived and as much as I'm sure I enjoyed it, acting and commercial auditions were awaiting me. Melissa and I performed our recital at a local college auditorium in front of an audience filled with friends and family members of all the dance students. For my one and only dance performance, I was dressed in a black satin leotard with three white puffy balls down the center, white fluffy feathers around the top of my bust-line and a white feathery tail attached to my behind. I wore black satin arm-length, open-fingered gloves that attached around my middle finger along with a white feathery headband that held up my sparkly black cat ears. I don't remember what music we tapped to; I can't even recall the recital itself, but the pictures with my sister in her equally adorable lime green leotard with my mom and dad and grandparents show me that it really did happen.

I also took a few ballroom dance lessons when I was sixteen as a present to my dad for his birthday. My dad, although not a very confident dancer, always took my hand and led me to the dance floor if a slow song was playing when we were at a party or wedding. I loved dancing with him, and even as a teenager it was one place I was never embarrassed to be seen with my parents. My dad loved watching his daughters have fun on the dance floor and his eyes were always beaming with pride and amusement, no matter how silly we looked doing the latest moves.

One year, wanting to give him an extra special birthday gift, I signed the two of us up for six ballroom dance classes at a professional studio. He was thrilled and I knew the end result would be moments and memories to cherish forever. For my wedding, my dad enlisted a choreographer who taught the two of us a special routine for our father/daughter dance, which included the waltz, disco, country, swing, and the YMCA. Our guests went crazy when we broke out of what everyone thought to be the start of a traditional dance to Nat King Cole's "What a Wonderful World" and into a mash-up of songs and moves that had everyone grooving on the dance floor by the end of it. I take full credit for starting what's now become the phenomenon of YouTube choreographed wedding dances!

But one recital, a few lessons with my dad, and a killer father/daughter wedding dance does not make me a professional dancer. Not by a long shot! I've been trained as an actress and spent much of my time in the laboratory of life learning how to be a wife and mom, but that didn't keep me from dreaming about standing on the *DWTS* stage.

Making a Scene

I was on an airplane flying to New York City when suddenly I had the urge to jump up and down and scream!

I was checking e-mail at 30,000 feet (thank you, Wi-Fi) when I got the offer. I had been officially invited to be a cast member on Season 18 of *Dancing with the Stars*.

I have turned down countless reality shows over the years. If you can name it, chances are, I've been asked to be on it. I've had no interest in being on shows that are all about cat fights, sex, drama, or resurrecting dead Hollywood careers. But after being glued to my TV watching the first season of *Dancing with the Stars*, I realized this one was different. It was a show I could imagine myself being on. It was a fun-spirited competition—in amazing sparkling, glittery costumes no less. And instead of creating a villain, stirring up rivalries, or seeking salacious plotlines, this show told stories about each contestant's journey. It seemed to focus on the best in people, even if that person wasn't the best at heart from the start, guiding them through something exciting yet scary and capturing all the moments in between. This was the one reality show I thought I would actually consider being a part of. Not to mention, my toes were still itching to learn how to really dance!

My husband, Val, knew how much I liked the show, considering I dedicated my Monday and Tuesday nights to watching as a fan in the early years of the show's run. I asked him what he thought if I were ever asked to be on the show, and without hesitation, he would say, "Do what makes you happy." Val's the kind of guy who has always supported my career decisions in entertainment, even though it's never been a personal area of interest for him. He believes in hard work and being passionate about what you do. So with that, he's always been my quiet champion cheering me on from the sidelines.

While I was on ABC Family's *Make It or Break It* from 2009 to 2012, my agents would receive regular calls from the show's producers asking for my availability to be on *DWTS*, but it never seemed to work out. This only grew my desire to be on the show even more and planted a seed not only to check it off my bucket list, but also to fulfill my inner "little girl" dream. It wasn't until Season 18 that all the cards fell in the right place. That's why I wanted to scream when I got the official invitation to be on the show! Only, I was on an airplane, with no one to tell but the man next to me! Except, I contractually couldn't tell anyone. As soon as I finished cheering and waving my arms in the air from my seat, I messaged Val from my computer. I managed to contain my excitement enough to avoid jumping up and screaming, but just barely. The guy next to me thought I was crazy, but I didn't care, I was so happy to see my dream finally come true.

True to form, Val was a cheerleader from the start. He said, "I'm so excited for you. I know you've wanted this forever."

With a longtime dream realized, and the support of my man, I nestled back into my seat and spent the rest of the flight dreaming of what was ahead.

Standing with Conviction

It was part of my contract with *DWTS*, that I kept my participation under wraps until the big cast reveal on *Good Morning America*. My daughter, Natasha, overheard a conversation between her dad and me about the show and put two and two together that I was on the cast list (smart girl!) and she was beyond excited. We eventually told the boys a week before the announcement as well as my best friend, Dilini, and friend Stacy who would help us with the kids during the busy schedule. But other than those few, no one knew before the cast was announced, not even my mom, sisters, or closest friends. I love surprises and couldn't wait to see them come unglued with excitement.

In that incubation period, when the realization of my dream was a close-kept secret, I felt nothing but happiness. I knew the show would stretch me mentally and physically, but I felt confident that I could face whatever was coming because I had the protection of Christ, the community of Christ, and the support of those closest to me.

But after the news broke, things got a little stickier.

My family was still super supportive. Natasha, Lev, Maks, and Val were just as jazzed as ever and many other family members and friends were excited and supportive too, but I started to hear expressions of concern.

"What if you're tempted to compromise?"

"Will you lose your conviction on the things you've taken a stand for?"

"What if the producers push you so hard and you feel pressured to give in to something that doesn't line up with God's Word?"

"Should a Christian be on a show about dancing?"

"What about the costumes? Aren't they a little too sexy?"

Well-meaning people, some from my inner circle, but many of whom I had never met, began expressing concern and frustration about my choice. It seemed like nearly everybody, aside from me, was worried that I had set myself up for failure. Certainly, I am human and capable of making mistakes and falling short of the marks God has for me. But conviction is the very reason I am still a woman of faith. It is the thing that grounds me in my faith. I can't live the Christian life and stay true to who I am in Christ and how He has called me to live without conviction. Another way to think of conviction is boundaries. I knew what my boundaries were before I ever agreed to participate in the show.

Where does my strong sense of conviction come from? From the Bible! By studying God's Word, I learn where God stands on issues and I seek to stand with Him. But there are gray areas, where the Bible doesn't lay out a boundary in black and white. In those cases, my conviction comes from the Holy Spirit in me.

First Corinthians 6:19 says it this way, "Don't you know that your body is a sanctuary of the Holy Spirit who is in you, whom you have from God? You are not your own."

The Holy Spirit lives within me! He guides me and nudges me to be more like Christ. But that's not my only compass. God has given me a community of people who care about me and want to see me live like Christ has called me to live. I know that when I need to draw a boundary that is not specifically outlined in the Bible, I can bounce my decisions off the most important people in my life to make sure I'm not acting on emotions or strong desires. Those important people are my husband and my mentors in my Christian faith including some of the women in my small group Bible study, my mom, my sisters, and a handful of other women that I know will be honest and truthful with me and are also grounded in the Word of God.

So, while others worried I might be pushed to jump outside of the boundaries God has for me, I knew I could say "yes" to this opportunity without fear of failure because I had the protection of Christ. I had the community of Christ. I had the prayers of my community, my family and friends in my fellowship, and I knew I was covered and protected no matter what the outcome. That was why I could step out in faith. It's also why you can step out in faith and do something out of your comfort zone.

In John 15:5 Jesus said, "I am the vine; you are the branches. The one who remains in Me and I in him produces much fruit, because you can do nothing without Me."

Apart from Jesus I probably couldn't have stood up for what I believed without wavering. I might not have had the courage to boldly share my faith with millions of people. Maybe I wouldn't have had the clarity to know what decisions to make along the way. But I wasn't on my own. I had Jesus! I had His Word. I had the encouragement and discernment of my community around me. I knew that if I could cling to Him through this journey, I could tackle the challenge that was in front of me.

What about you?

What do you "cling" to when you are in a season of being stretched? How do you decide where your boundaries are? As you read my story, let me encourage you to look at your own heart and wrestle with the concept of conviction, because if you don't know where your boundaries are before you are thrown into a challenging situation, you are almost guaranteed to fall flat on your face.

The apostle Paul wrote about this reality in Ephesians 6:10–17 when he was describing the armor of God. I'd encourage you to check out the entire passage, but let me highlight three places where Paul wrote about standing with conviction.

Finally, be strengthened by the Lord and by His vast strength. Put on the full armor of God so that you can stand against the tactics of the Devil. (vv. 10–11)

We can be strong because of the Lord's strength. We can stand with conviction because of the protection and guidance He offers us.

This is why you must take up the full armor of God, so that you may be able to resist in the evil day, and having prepared everything, to take your stand. (v. 13)

Standing firm is what conviction is all about. I knew that I could be confident that I would stand firm in my convictions through this journey, not because of my own strength, but because of the strength that God freely offers me.

In verse 14, Paul repeats his order to stand: "Stand, therefore, with truth like a belt around your waist, righteousness like armor on your chest."

I knew that because of God's Word, I was anchored in truth. I knew that because of my faith in Christ, I was protected from harm even as I entered this season of stretching. None of that meant the journey would be easy, but I knew I could stand with conviction, even with millions of eyes watching, because I would be clinging to the Vine the whole time.

I'm sure you've heard it said that if you don't stand for something, you will fall for anything. That's exactly what Paul is preaching in this passage. If we don't hold our lives together with God's truth, we will never be able to stand firm. If we don't know what our convictions are before the challenge comes, the world will decide them for us and we are destined to compromise. I knew that I could use the platform I had been given to stand for what I believed, because my convictions were firmly decided ahead of time.

Maybe my journey can help you think through your own boundaries. Where do your convictions come from? To whom or what do you look to help you determine what you will stand for?

The Reality of Reality TV

Soon enough it was time to get down to business. The premise of the show is that each celebrity is matched with a professional dancer. I didn't know who my pro partner was until he showed up at my house while the cameras rolled.

I was secretly rooting for Mark Ballas or Val Chmerkovskiy to be my partner. I had a dream the week before the initial meeting that was simply a face . . . which was Val's face (the dancer, not my husband) so I thought I might be getting a glimpse of who I'd be paired up with. I was excited at this prospect because I knew he was an incredible dancer, I liked his personality from what I'd seen on the show, and size wise I thought we were a good fit. But when I imagined myself on the show over the years, I always thought I'd most likely be paired up with Mark. I liked Mark, he was fun and goofy and not too intense. And looking back through some of his other partners, I always felt like he'd be the one for me. So I was thrilled when I opened the door to find Mark standing on my doorstep.

Right away, as we filmed the very first segment for the show, I had an opportunity to stand with conviction. Mark asked me several questions like what my expectations were of the show, how much dance experience I had, and what I was most nervous about. Without really even thinking about it (that's what happens when your boundaries are set ahead of time), I said that I didn't want to be cast as "the sexy girl." I'm a mom of three kids. I knew that I didn't want to sell sex for the sake of getting me further on the show. I said up front that I wanted to have the opportunity to look classy and feel beautiful. I even said that I wanted my costumes to be on the more modest side, a boundary that would certainly be put to the test in the weeks ahead.

Then it was time to get to work. Mark and I started practicing four hours a day, seven days a week in the practice studio. At this stage in the game, we were only allowed to practice for four hours in order to give our bodies time to adjust to the physical demands of the show. But it sure didn't feel like much of an adjustment period! We hit the ground running, and running hard!

Suddenly, I had to juggle being a wife and a mom of three kids while seizing a once-in-a-lifetime opportunity. One of the first emotions to hit me during this process was a wave of mom guilt. I knew that the show was going to require me to be away from my kids a lot even though I was still in Los Angeles. It was tough knowing I'd be here, but I wouldn't be very available for them.

I had the dream. Now I had the opportunity to do it, but there was a tiny tug-of-war happening in my heart. Because of my kids, there were times I wondered if it was okay to pursue my dream. I wondered if I was being selfish by doing something that would require my family to step out

> To help maintain my weight and to avoid stress about preparing meals, I used a food service throughout the duration of the show that delivered three meals and two snacks to my door daily. I ate an average of 1,500 calories a day.

of their comfort zones too, and I wrestled with how to know if this was something God really wanted me to do.

This certainly wasn't the first time I had experienced mom guilt. Even if you're not a mom, you likely know that as women, prioritizing can be tough. We often face choices where we have to weigh an opportunity on one side of the scale and the potential impact on the people we care about on the other. Will my kids be okay if I work these long hours? Will my parents be disappointed if I chase my own dream instead of the dream they have for me? Will my friends be hurt if I invest my time and energy into this project for a season, leaving less time to invest in our friendship?

I had to think through how to cope with mom guilt while pursuing a personal dream. Ultimately, I jumped over that hurdle by focusing on what I want my children to learn from me. I don't want to nurture my children into being unable or unwilling to be stretched out of their comfort zones. I don't want my kids to be afraid to take the opportunities God gives them and use them to point others toward Him. I don't just want my kids to hear what the Bible says; I want them to see it in action.

Philippians 4:13 promises: "I am able to do all things through Him who strengthens me."

I knew that was true, and I wanted my kids to see it through my life!

I also knew that I had my husband's support every step of the way. Val has always been a hands-on dad. He's never been one of

> Natasha came with me to rehearsal most Saturdays and gave me "face tips."

those guys who shies away from changing a diaper, driving carpool, coaching the kids in sports, making breakfast, lunch, and dinner, having heart-to-heart conversations with them, or doing whatever needs to be done. He's always been a very involved parent, and while the show would require him to kick his role into hyper drive—something he's done many times before when I've filmed out of town—I knew that our kids would be well taken care of and supported. That's not to say the guilt didn't come and go. Sometimes, I think that's just part of being a woman, but ultimately, I could lay it down because I knew that my kids were watching me be stretched beyond my comfort zone.

Lights, Camera, Action

Once practices started, the cameras were rolling constantly. All of our practices were filmed by a crew of at least two people—one producer operating the camera and one person sitting at the computer operating the sound and making editing notes. Since I had been acting since I was five years old, I was pretty used to the cameras, but I wasn't used to the spotlight being quite so constant. The cameras were literally on all the time from the minute we walked in the doors!

Mark was a patient teacher and I needed his patience! As it turns out, those childhood dance lessons didn't carry me very far in a competition with professional dancers and gold-medalist athletes. Very early on, my mind and body were being stretched in new ways. I even got some major bruises during practice those first couple of weeks. I considered them battle scars and shared photos of them on my weekly blog on *People* magazine's website. I had a lot to learn if I was going to compete on this stage, but I felt ready for the challenge.

Our first live show was right around the corner. I didn't know it, but I had just strapped in for the ride of my life!

Chapter 2

Going All In

"Come!" He said. And climbing out of the boat, Peter
started walking on the water and came toward Jesus.
—MATTHEW 14:29

There's a famous story in the Bible where Jesus and one of
His disciples walked on water. Matthew 14:22–33 tells us
that Jesus sent His friends across the Sea of Galilee while He
retreated alone to pray. A storm blew up and the boat Jesus'
friends were on was beaten and tossed by the wind.

Suddenly, they peeked out of their battered ship to see
someone walking on the water toward them. They were
afraid. I would be too if I saw someone floating toward me
without a boat! Not to mention that the disciples' nerves were
already standing at attention as their little boat struggled to
stay afloat in a nasty storm.

But Jesus never gets anxious. His nerves never get the best of Him. While the disciples freaked out, Jesus stayed calm.

"Immediately Jesus spoke to them. 'Have courage! It is I. Don't be afraid'" (v. 27).

I know what it's like to ride through choppy waters. Only two weeks into my *Dancing with the Stars* experience, I felt a lot like that little boat. Rehearsals had left me literally bruised over much of my body and I was exhausted! At one point in those early weeks, I took my kids out for frozen yogurt and fell fast asleep on a bench while they ate. I was just too tired to keep my eyes open!

Our first live show was just days away. Sure, I had some butterflies about dancing in front of millions of people for the first time, but I also felt ready to take the leap. In fact, I approached that first show with much of the same fearlessness that I had accepted the offer to be on *DWTS* in the first place. I didn't know exactly what that first live show would be like, but I was ready to step out of the boat and see if I would sink or swim.

Speaking of sinking, that's exactly what Peter did in the story I was just telling you about. Right after Jesus told His disciples not to be afraid, Peter made a gutsy request.

> "Lord, if it's You," Peter answered Him, "command me to come to You on the water."
>
> "Come!" He said.
>
> And climbing out of the boat, Peter started walking on the water and came toward Jesus. But when he saw the strength of the wind, he was afraid. And beginning to sink he cried out, "Lord, save me!"

Immediately Jesus reached out His hand, caught hold of him, and said to him, "You of little faith, why did you doubt?" (vv. 28–31)

Being on *DWTS* wasn't exactly water-walking, but as the first live show approached, the risks that come with stepping out of my comfort zone were on my mind. When fear rose up or the ground felt a little unsteady underneath my feet, I was reminded that sometimes God calls us to take risks because it makes us dependent on Him, just like when Jesus encouraged Peter to step out of the boat onto the choppy waves of a stormy sea. I was convinced that I was about to see Him move in ways I never would have if I had played it safe, and I was right!

Going All In

We found out early on that our first dance would be contemporary. In case you're a dance novice (like me!), let me give you a crash course in contemporary dance. Contemporary is a style of expressive dance that combines elements of several genres like modern, jazz, lyrical, and classical ballet. Contemporary dance isn't as strict or as structured as other dances. The emphasis is on fluid movements. While there was plenty of technique to learn, I felt like the first dance played to my strengths. It helped that Mark was a patient teacher. We were working hard but I was having so much fun.

One thing Mark emphasized often as we rehearsed was that I needed to give 100 percent every single time we practiced our dance. That was a foreign concept to me, because as an actress I've been trained to hold back. During rehearsals for a show or movie, I might give 70 to 80 percent in order to save my energy and emotion for when the cameras are roll-ing, but Mark kept telling me that's not how it works in the dance world. He needed to know exactly how I was going to perform in the live show. He told me that if I was going to push harder when the cameras were rolling, that he needed to know so that he could adjust his resistance. He instructed me not to hold anything back for the performance in rehears-als. I couldn't save anything. Part of training to be a dancer was learning to give everything I had every single time we rehearsed. That was hard for me! It was something that Mark and I struggled through during the entire show.

As with so much about this journey, this was a lesson about more than dancing. Long before *DWTS*, I had commit-ted to making my faith my number-one priority in my life, but it was as if God was giving me an object lesson on how important it was to give Him 100 percent all of the time. Giving God everything is such a critical part of the Christian walk. Jesus asks us to love Him with *all* of our heart, soul, mind, and strength (Luke 10:27). We believe that *all* of the Bible is true and useful for our lives (2 Tim. 3:16). We seek to surrender *every* area of our lives to God's control. In faith, as in every area, a partial commitment ruins the whole thing. If I'm only halfway committed to my marriage, the partnership won't work. I must be all in. If I'm only partway invested in my children, my job as a mother isn't complete. And if I'm only giving Jesus 70 to 80 percent of my life, my heart, my resources, I'm not living the way He has called me to live. As Mark was training me to give 100 percent every time I danced, the Lord was reminding me that He asks me to give Him 100 percent too. While I naturally wanted to hold back my best efforts for when the cameras were rolling, Mark was showing me that I needed to go all in, even when it was just me and him and the producers in a rehearsal studio.

In the same way, sometimes we are tempted to live our lives for Jesus only when others are watching, but there was another clear parallel. Yes, God had given me this platform upon which I could live out my convictions, but being a follower of Jesus means living my life for Him at all times, even when no one is watching.

Remember Peter and his battered boat? When his eyes were on Jesus and he focused on his Savior 100 percent, nothing could touch him. The storm was raging, the waves were churning, but he had set his course and he was walking on that choppy water! When he pulled back . . . when he tried to focus on Jesus *and* what was going on around him . . . when his trust level dropped down below 100 percent, he started to sink.

I wanted to learn to give 100 percent on the dance floor and in every other area of my life. So I kept practicing!

Gearing Up for the Big Show

Lots of people have asked me how the elements of each show are chosen. The producers pick the type of dance each couple does each week. Every couple doesn't necessarily do every type of dance during the season, and certainly some types of dances are more difficult than others. I was thrilled to have been assigned a dance genre that came a little more naturally to me for the first week.

The other elements of the show are a result of collaboration. Mark and I had the chance to sit down with the producers and give them a list of songs we would like to dance to. Since Mark's ear is much more trained to hear music as a dancer than mine is, he was a natural at matching the songs we both liked with a category of dance. (I just knew what made me want to move!) Ultimately, the producers chose the song for us, but they took our requests into consideration and tried to accommodate them as best as possible. If, for some reason, our choice conflicted with approval rights for playing the song on TV, or another contestant's choice, it's at the producers' discretion to choose something for us. For week one, we got the song "Burn" by Ellie Goulding, a song Mark had submitted, and I was very happy to dance to such a popular and current song I already loved.

Costuming was also a group effort. In addition to setting the standard that I wanted my costumes to reflect who I am as a woman while the cameras were rolling the first time I met Mark, I also had conversations with the wardrobe department early on about it. They gave me the freedom to choose costumes that were as modest or as revealing as I felt comfortable with. They told me, "We want everyone to feel great and comfortable because ultimately if you don't feel good out there in your costume, you're not going to perform well, so the costumes are at your discretion." Honestly, I had no fear of the costume department and didn't have a clue at this point in the journey that what I wore during live shows would become such a focus of debate!

For the first week of competition, my costume was a white, beaded, tank bodice with a flowing turquoise blue, layered skirt designed to show off all of that strong, controlled leg movement Mark and I had been working on. Wardrobe was just one part of the production that really started to ramp up as the live show got closer and closer. Before I knew it, it was the Monday of our first show!

Going LIVE

I know that as a spectator, the live show looks like one big party! Maybe that's why I've been a fan of the show for so long; but as a participant, I soon realized the day of the show was grueling. The show was filmed on Mondays and it was a jam-packed day!

On the day of the live show I left my house by 6:30 a.m. to be on set by 7:15 a.m. The makeup chair was my first stop. Imagine getting false lashes applied first thing in the morning with enough glue to make them stick for twelve hours! Midway through makeup, the producers came to pull me out of the chair for camera blocking. That's when we ran through the routine for the cameras. This allows the cameramen to set their final positions and camera shots before the official dress rehearsal. After blocking, I headed back to the makeup chair and then the stylists started on my hair. It didn't take me long to figure out that those forty-five minutes in the hair-styling chair provided a great opportunity to read my Bible. The pace of the rest of the day was so intense that I needed that time in the Word to help me focus on what was really important. This is a lesson I think applies to all of life. The pace of life is often so fast, we don't always have time to pause and spend time with the Lord. We must take advantage of the time we do have so His Word is stored in our hearts and can be our fuel in the busyness of life.

> Did you know that *DWTS* shares a two-soundstage building with *American Idol*? I occasionally said hello to Randy Jackson in the hallways and got a chance to wave at JLo and some of the contestants.

Once my hair was done, it was time for lunch. On show days, I couldn't seem to stomach much food because I was so nervous and didn't want to get an unexpected sour stomach from anything, so I ate light. From lunch we moved into a full dress rehearsal with costumes and all. Dress rehearsal started at 1:00 p.m. and we were literally running through the show in its exact timing of how it would be live. In addition to giving us the chance to get our bearings for what was ahead, the dress rehearsal allows producers to make sure that everything fits within the scheduled frame, because the show really is live. What you see is what you get, leaving no room for errors.

That first dress rehearsal flew by and in no time at all it was 4:40. The entire cast and crew was on stage and I felt like I was in the center of a beehive. The stage was literally buzzing with activity! The audience had been packed into the studio. There were celebrities backstage. A team of ten hairdressers and ten makeup artists were doing last-minute touch-ups on everyone. People were stretching and each couple still had their own camera crew filming their every move. It was chaos!

> Someone asked Mark and me, "What happens if you need to take a potty break right before the show?" Here's how we answered.
>
> *Mark:* You gotta hold it!
>
> *Me:* I always plan it out. I'm a mom. Potty breaks are always scheduled!

Live television was a whole new ball game for me. As a TV and movie actor, I've always been able to stop and start again if I mess up. I have never performed theatre, not even a school play! If I could describe that moment in one word, it would be *overwhelming*. As the competition progressed, I got used to the buzz, but at first I was totally and completely overwhelmed by it. I didn't have time to focus on those feelings for long, because it was almost time to put all of that practice to work for my first-ever dance in front of an audience. And it just happened to be an audience of millions!

At 4:55 we were in position on the stage. The BBC and ABC logo came up and we were live, baby!

A High Bar

Our first dance was amazing! Looking back, those two minutes on stage before our dance while the video package was being played and our one minute and fifteen seconds of actual dancing are a bit of a blur, but I remember thinking, *This is it! I'm actually doing it. I'm gonna go for it! I'm gonna have fun and relax.* And I recalled each and every step of my whole routine in my mind and tried to remember everything Mark told me to do, even down to my facial expressions. I felt like an Olympic athlete about to compete for the first time and I didn't want to miss anything. And I didn't! It went as well as I could have hoped and I knew Mark would be pleased with me. Then it was time to face the judges. I didn't know exactly what to expect, but the judges' words were so encouraging! They added to the high I was already feeling from accomplishing my goal of dancing well in front of all of those people.

Len said, "You can dance. Well done." Bruno called me a contemporary dancer. Me? A girl whose dancing experience had previously been limited to a childhood recital in a cat costume and a few fun wedding dances? Carrie Ann asked me where those moves had come from. "You are such an incredible dancer," she said. "I want to see it again!"

I was on cloud nine. I was out of the boat, walking toward my dream with my eyes focused on Jesus and I wasn't sinking! I felt so much pride in myself for tackling something I had never done before—and to top it off, I got the first 9 of the night along with two 8s for a total of 25 out of 30 points, placing me second at the top of the leaderboard!

The Faces behind the Scenes

I'm not sure I could have made it through that first show without the support of my family and friends. If you watched the show, you might have caught a glimpse of Val and the kids and a few friends who came to the taping. Each celebrity was given eight tickets per show. The producers were strict about the number of guests we could invite. They would not give us more than those eight tickets. If I could have bent that rule, I would have. I wanted everyone I knew to watch my *DWTS* debut!

The faces you didn't see were the people cheering me on from beyond the *DWTS* stage. Starting with that very first show, I had two prayer teams in place led by my friend Clare Smith. Clare is a fitness blogger I met several years ago when I launched a website called Roo Magazine. Clare was recommended to

During the show I was often asked why my brother, Kirk, wasn't in the audience. Between his six active kids' schedules and his touring conference schedule, Monday nights simply didn't work out for him or his family to be in the audience. However, my parents, two sisters, and grandmother were all able to come various weeks and I felt well supported by my entire family.

me as a health and fitness writer and joined my team. Because of our shared love for health, fitness, food, and cute clothes, Clare and I clicked instantly. She's become a close friend. I've since taken Roo Magazine down, but my friendship with Clare and several of the other members of my writing team remains. When Clare learned I would be on *DWTS*, she offered to host a prayer team for me. She asked me for a list of individuals I wanted her to include on the prayer team and suggested we break the names into two groups. The first was an intimate group of prayer partners that she could e-mail the specific details of my prayer needs. That became a tight circle of women who prayed faithfully for me throughout the entire journey. Clare also organized a larger group of about thirty ladies who I trusted to pray for me in more general terms.

Clare sent out regular prayer updates to those two teams. She would often direct them to pray a certain passage of Scripture for me and would ask me daily how the groups could pray for me. I sure needed those prayers as I faced the first live show, and as the journey continued my prayer team became an absolute lifeline. They prayed me through that first show and they were right there cheering for me as it wrapped. The feedback from that first show was very positive. My phone blew up with texts of encouragement and people saying, "Way to go!"

All of that fed into my high, but as I looked down from that mountain of excitement and pride and support, I started to worry about the next round of competition. I was proud of myself for conquering my fears and was thrilled that Mark and I had hit one out of the park, but almost immediately I started to fear I had set the bar too high for myself. I don't like disappointing people and I was suddenly afraid that I wouldn't be able to live up to the expectations of others. I wanted room

Here's an insider's peek into Clare's "recruitment letter" that she used to launch my prayer team:

Friends and Family of Candace,

It is with great excitement that we usher Candace into a fun, new season of life as she is on *Dancing with the Stars*! We know this has been a dream of hers for a while now, so to see it come to reality is quite a blessing! What a fun week we had watching her perform and the outpouring of support from her fans!

A part of Candace's testimony is Esther 4:14. "For if you remain silent at this time, relief and deliverance for the Jews will arise from another place, but you and your father's family will perish. And who knows but that you have come to your royal position for such a time as this?" (NIV). For such a time as this—and this is most definitely a "time"! As she does the works that God has put in advance for her to do, with the gifts He's given her, and the place in the body of Christ that He has placed her, the time is now! We need to rally around our sister as she cannot do it alone!

to grow as a dancer and a woman, and I was afraid that the judges and the public were going to expect too much of me going forward. They would expect me to improve, but the bar had already been set so high. Just like Peter went from walking on the water to sinking like a stone in an instant, my fears and anxieties started to pull me down.

Proceed with Caution: Stormy Waters Ahead

Like so much of my *DWTS* journey, learning to ride the peaks and valleys of the show mirrored my Christian walk.

For many Christians, coming to Jesus is a spiritual high. It is exciting! The love and acceptance of Jesus is awesome and overwhelming. At first, it is so easy to want to share Jesus with everybody, but it doesn't take long to hit a roadblock.

I cringe when I hear someone preach that people should come and try Jesus because He will improve their life. They promise peace and joy and love, and I've seen new believers grab on to that with both hands, expecting God to be the genie that makes their life easy. While it's true that peace, joy, and love are gifts that God loves to give His children, He never promises that our lives will be problem-free. When we don't understand that truth, we can be alarmed and upset when life gets hard. I've heard new believers say, "I thought God was supposed to make my life better!" But that's not why we come to Christ. We come to Him because we are great sinners and He is a great Savior.

Remember that story of Peter walking on the water toward Jesus? The Bible does not say that Jesus calmed the storm before He invited Peter to step out of the boat. The storm was still raging. The waves were still crashing. That water was still churning! But Jesus was with His friends in the midst of the storm.

As that first show ended, I couldn't help but wonder if I was sailing toward stormy waters. I didn't want to be a one-hit wonder. It was so exciting to get high scores and to feel the love of my friends and fans, but I immediately felt the pressure of setting the bar so high.

The only way I could stay afloat was the same way Peter did. I kept my eyes on Jesus. I determined to walk as He had called me to do, pressing on with my eyes on Him.

Chapter 3

The Gritty Side of Salt and Light

But the LORD said to Samuel, "Do not look at his appearance or his stature, because I have rejected him. Man does not see what the LORD sees, for man sees what is visible, but the LORD sees the heart."
—1 SAMUEL 16:7

WARNING: Standing with conviction takes courage!

There was no time to catch my breath after the first show. When the sun came up the day after that triumphant first live performance, Mark and I headed back into the rehearsal studio for the next round of competition. It turned out to be a leg of my *DWTS* journey that proved that standing with conviction isn't always easy or popular.

In an interview for the show on that first day I met Mark, the producers asked me what dance I wanted to do most. I drew a total blank! To be honest, because of my inexperience as a dancer, at that point I simply didn't know the difference between a fox-trot and a cha-cha. Natasha piped up and suggested that I pick a rumba or a samba. I'm not sure she knew what those dances looked like at that point either, but I said, "Sure! I really want to do the rumba." Note to self: don't let your teenage daughter pick your favorite dance! Especially if it's one you'll be dancing live on national television, in front of millions of people.

It turns out that the rumba is one of the toughest ballroom dances to master. In that first day of practices, Mark described the rumba to me as "the dance of love." It is designed to be a romantic dance, characterized by slow, sensual hip movements. Mark was worried because of the difficultly of the dance in the second week of competition. I was worried for different reasons. I knew that I wanted to represent Christ well and I wanted to honor my husband. I had already made the decision that I wouldn't sell sex for the sake of getting further on the show. I had made up my mind, and stated publicly, that I wanted to be modest because of my roles as wife and mom and because I knew from the Word that modesty mattered to God. But, this was a sexy dance! How could I do a routine designed to showcase sexuality and still stand with conviction?

Can I shoot straight with you? Standing with conviction isn't easy. Going with the flow and bending to the standards of the world around me would have been a much smoother path. I didn't go on *DWTS* to crusade for my faith or to take a stand for modesty, but I was determined to be true to who I am. I am a Christian. I am a happily married woman who desires to reserve some parts of my life and my body for my husband. I am someone who wants to showcase Christ in the way that I live and dress. It wasn't always easy to be true to those parts of my identity on *DWTS*, but let's face it, Easy Street doesn't always take us where we want to be anyway.

In fact, James 1:2–4 encourages us to consider it a great joy when the road gets rocky, "Consider it a great joy, my brothers, whenever you experience various trials, knowing that the testing of your faith produces endurance. But endurance must do its complete work, so that you may be mature and complete, lacking nothing."

This week of the competition tested my willingness to truly stand with conviction. But that testing led to steadfastness—an unswerving, unflinching, unwavering commitment to live according to God's Word. My time on *DWTS* is only a small part of my story. Over and over I learned that this was not a journey about dancing or about being on a television show. This was about learning to live with conviction in all areas of my life. When the cameras were on and when they were off. When the public was behind me and when they weren't. When I was wearing my celebrity hat and when I was wearing the hats of wife, mom, sister, daughter, and friend. James was right, while the testing of my faith sometimes felt like a trial, complete with a judge and jury, I loved the opportunity to live what I believed in front of the watching world.

Making Adjustments

Early in the week, Mark brought me into the studio to show me the dance he choreographed for us to perform. Every pro choreographs differently. Some choreograph while simultaneously teaching the moves to their celebrity partner.

Mark tended to do the choreography on his own and then show me the finished product using another pro partner.

The dance he choreographed for the rumba was beautiful! True to rumba style, it was a very slow, sensual dance. It clearly told the story of the roller coaster ride that romantic relationships can sometimes be. Performed to A Great Big World's, "Say Something," it was a very emotional and beautiful piece. I literally cried when Mark showed me the choreography. I felt like he was telling such a passionate story and I got sucked right into its depths!

At the very end of the dance, there was a particularly beautiful and poignant move that made me catch my breath after seeing it and gave me a little tingle inside. I wondered if I was just taken from the emotion of the dance, or if there was something more to it. I had videotaped that first dance so that I could rewatch the moves later that night, burning them into my memory. As I was watching the tape at home, I had another pause in my spirit at the end of the dance. I wondered if the maneuver was too sexy or if it would be perceived in a way that didn't match up with who I am as a wife, a mom, and a woman.

Do you remember how I told you my convictions are determined? My first litmus test is God's Word.

I knew that the Bible commanded me to honor my husband (Eph. 5:33) and to present myself in a way that is respectable and modest (1 Tim. 2:8–10). I wanted to live out those principles because they were clear in God's Word. But what did that look like, exactly? What did respecting Val look like in the context of a sensual dance on a reality television show? What does modesty mean exactly? Is it just about clothing, or did it extend into the way I carried myself on and off the dance floor?

In a situation where the Bible does not clearly outline the choice I should make, I ask the Holy Spirit to inform my convictions. I believe that little hesitation in my heart about the dance move at the end of the routine was a nudge from the Holy Spirit.

I told you in chapter 1 that I make choices based on what God's Word says, what I sense the Holy Spirit is saying to my heart, *and* through the discernment and encouragement of wise people in my life. In this situation, Val played an active role in helping me think through my choices on the show, just like he does in "real life." I showed him the tape of the rumba without letting him know about my concerns on the last move. He watched the dance and when it got to the move in question he said, "I don't like that last move. I'm not sure it will be perceived well." My response was, "Okay. Good. That was the one I was hesitating about, so if you feel that way too I will ask Mark to change it."

The Bible helped me know the importance of respecting my husband. The Holy Spirit nudged me that one element of the dance might not be perceived as doing that. So, I took it to my community—in this case, that was specifically my husband—and he lovingly encouraged me to make a change. The result was a conviction, or a decision, that part of the dance wasn't a good fit for who I am and what I stand for. As a result, I asked Mark to change it. He honored that and adjusted the dance to make me more comfortable.

What Submission Really Looks Like

I've taken some heat for saying publicly that I believe the Bible calls me to submit to the leadership of my husband. The match that ignited that fire came from my book *Balancing It All.*

> My husband is a natural-born leader. I quickly learned that I had to find a way of honoring his take-charge personality and not get frustrated about his desire to have the final decision on just about everything. I am not a passive person, but I chose to fall into a more submissive role in our relationship because I wanted to do everything in my power to make my marriage and family work.[1]

That word *submissive* was talked about everywhere from *The View* to national news outlets like CNN and Fox and every magazine and blog in between after the book was released. That doesn't surprise me. I recognize that we live in a culture where many see submission as old-fashioned and out-of-date. But my beliefs aren't informed by the ever-changing winds of culture. My commitment to submission inside the context of marriage comes straight from God's Word. (Recognize a pattern here?) Ephesians 5:22–24 says, "Wives, submit to your own husbands as to the Lord, for the husband is the head of the wife as Christ is the head of the church. He is the Savior of the body. Now as the church submits to Christ, so wives are to submit to their husbands in everything."

The picture that's painted here is beautiful! Women are to submit, or defer, to their husbands as a picture of our relationship with Christ. We surrender our lives to Him. We bend to His leadership in our lives. We hand over the reins and let Him lead. While I don't do it perfectly, I can showcase what a life surrendered to Christ looks like through my marriage! But if you stop reading there, you miss part of the picture. I am convinced that the reason the culture reacts so strongly to this idea is because they only see half of the image God intends to draw through marriage.

Ephesians 5:25 reveals the rest of the story: "Husbands, love your wives, just as Christ loved the church and gave Himself for her."

Yes, the Bible urges me to submit to the leadership of my husband as an extension of my submission to Christ's leadership in my life, but it also asks Val to love me in the same way that Christ loves the church. If you think submission is countercultural, look around and try to find sacrificial love! The Bible encourages Val to love me with the same kind of costly love that Jesus gives me. Since He died to pay the penalty for my sins, I'd say that's a pretty tall order.

Even though these passages do inform the way Val and I treat each other, they aren't just a list of rules. They're much bigger than that. When we follow God's plan for marriage— when Val loves me sacrificially, following the example of Christ, and when I submit to his leadership as an extension of submitting my life to Jesus—we are painting a beautiful picture. We are a living exhibit of what Christ's love for His people looks like in action.

Deciding what I would and would not do during my *DWTS* journey is an example of what these principles can look like in real time. Val wasn't handing down absolutes. He was supportive and loving, always championing my dream. But when he saw something that might not work to my benefit, he spoke up. I wasn't a renegade, determined to do whatever I wanted without his insight. I talked to him at every step of the journey, asking for his opinion. Ultimately, I wanted to make choices that he and I were both proud of.

Because this is a rhythm that we've embraced as part of our faith, making the choice to alter the rumba together wasn't a big deal. We are a team and a true partnership. We want what's best for each other, and I was happy to go to Mark with my concerns even though I knew how much pride he takes in his choreography. Asking Mark to change it could have gone another way, but it didn't. He respected me and was a class act, changing the move without hesitation.

But the rumba battle didn't end there! Who knew the dance of love could feel like a war? During conversations with the costuming department at the beginning of the week, Mark said that he wanted to go shirtless for this dance. Remember that I said that I wanted to be modest in front of millions of people in that first show? I believe strongly that modesty is about so much more than what we wear or don't wear (more on that in a minute!), but Mark's proposed wardrobe choice didn't fit into my definition so I pushed back. In the video package that aired with the live show, I sounded pretty peeved at everyone including Mark about him being shirtless, but only after I felt like I was being joked about a little too long. It was all in good fun, but this was a real concern of mine and I didn't want to be dismissed. So, I took the opportunity to say again that my life revolves around my relationship with Jesus Christ and I wanted that to be portrayed and made sure my voice was heard, having input in all our decisions, making them together.

In the end, I was proud of the rumba Mark and I performed. The dance told a beautiful story of sensuality as opposed to raunchy sexuality. Our costumes fit a definition of modesty that was cohesive with my understanding of God's heart on the issue. And that dance was hard! While I didn't do it perfectly, I learned a very difficult dance and felt I performed it as well as I could. And as Mark's mom said to me several times, "God loves a trier! Now, get on with it."

"I'm a Sexual Woman!"

Ultimately, Mark and I didn't score well in this round of the competition. We ended up with 7s across the board. The judges criticized the extension of my arms and picked up on the fact that the hip movement was difficult for me. I don't know if it was the difficulty of the dance as much as it was allowing myself to let go without feeling disrespectful to my husband. But I knew that despite giving it my best, I didn't really encapsulate what a rumba is. To be honest, it was kind of a crash and burn, but I felt more relieved than anything. That high bar that terrified me from the week before had been lowered and I felt greater freedom to improve going forward.

There wasn't much time to rest in that relief, though. In the live interview after our dance, cohost Erin Andrews wanted to know how I merged my faith with the dance of love.

Erin: You talked a lot in the package about balancing your religious beliefs with a dance that's sexy, with a show that's sexy. How do you do it?

Me: I feel like a sexual woman. I've been married for eighteen years. I am a sexual woman, but I want to reserve certain things for my husband, so we did, I think, the best that we could with a rumba I still felt comfortable doing.

Other than declaring my faith in Jesus Christ, that brief interaction became the most talked about part of my *DWTS* experience. For the most part, response to my statement was overwhelmingly positive. My Twitter feed and Facebook page blew up with comments from other women saying things like:

- "Thank you for showing you can be a Christian and not a prude!"

- "Thanks for saying that we as Christian women are sexual beings."
- "It's because we want to save some things for our husbands that we don't have to let it all hang out."
- "Thanks for showcasing that God created sex as a gift!"
- "I am thankful for your candor. I see you as a role model for my teenage daughters who often hear a warped view of sex."

While the response was overwhelmingly positive, some people expressed genuine concern. Online and through my social media networks some people worried out loud that it was not a safe thing for me to be dancing a sensual dance with a man who is not my husband. Some argued that my public stance to live out my faith while on the show and my commitment to modesty were in conflict, specifically with this dance.

Heading into the live show where I would dance the rumba, I knew there was the potential for me to ignite a firestorm of controversy. Remember those praying friends? I depended on them heavily, especially when I sensed that my convictions might not be universally received. During this week of competition I specifically asked them to pray that the modesty I portrayed on stage would be a good

> Did you know that married, Christian women are among the most sexually satisfied women? It's true! A study conducted by the University of Chicago found that the most sexually satisfied women in the U.S. are middle-aged, married, church-going gals! Some have dubbed that study "the revenge of the church ladies"![2]

reflection of Christ and not lead to division in the body of Christ (a.k.a. the church), even if it didn't fit the mold of what everyone thought I should or should not be doing. Those girls got busy praying, and God answered them by opening up a dialogue about what His standards really look like.

What Is Modesty Exactly?

I already knew that the opinions of others outside of my community weren't good building blocks for my personal convictions. But their concerns helped me vet my own beliefs. I had to ask myself, what is modesty, exactly? What specific parameters are outlined for us in God's Word?

Modesty is a word found only a couple of times in Scripture. One of the most famous passages on the subject is 1 Timothy 2:9–10. The apostle Paul is writing to Timothy, a young pastor of a growing church when he says, "Also, the women are to dress themselves in modest clothing, with decency and good sense, not with elaborate hairstyles, gold, pearls, or expensive apparel, but with good works, as is proper for women who affirm that they worship God."

This passage says that women of faith should be modest, but what is modesty exactly? We tend to reduce the conversation about modesty to a list of rules about what we should or should not wear, but the Bible doesn't do that. Yes, this is a passage about what it should look like to be a woman of faith, but it's not a dress code. There's no hem length mentioned here. No black-and-white rules about sleeves or no sleeves or the exact right place for a Christian woman's neckline. In fact, this verse is less about the kind of clothing we wear and more about God's intention that we clothe ourselves with qualities that reflect Him.

Notice that right after Paul tells Timothy that women should dress modestly and avoid appearances designed to draw attention, that he makes it clear what all women of faith should wear—"decency and good sense." Obviously, those aren't things that hang in my closet! But I can make sure that when people look at me, they see me doing good things for others rather than trying to grab all of the attention for myself. This is just a puzzle piece in the bigger picture of God's heart for modesty presented in His Word.

- Matthew 6:28–30 tells us not to be preoccupied with clothes, but instead to focus on the things of God.
- 1 Corinthians 6:19–20 says that my body is a temple of the Holy Spirit. Therefore, I am called to honor God with my body.
- 1 Peter 3:3–4 says that true beauty is internal. Nothing I could ever put on and nothing I could ever take off can give me the kind of true, lasting beauty that comes from Christ working in me.
- 1 Peter 5:5–6 urges us to clothe ourselves with humility.
- Proverbs 31:25 describes a woman who is clothed in strength and dignity (ESV).
- Psalm 132:9 talks about being clothed with righteousness.

Instead of passing down a list of rules for what I wear, the Bible encourages me to "wear" the qualities of Christ. While costuming became one front where I repeatedly had the opportunity to stand with conviction on the show, I knew that making choices about what I would or wouldn't wear wasn't the most important way to showcase my identity in Christ. I needed to consistently "clothe" myself in the things that Christ modeled and then called me to—holiness, true beauty, humility, strength, dignity, and righteousness.

While online chatter tended to focus on what I wore, I wanted to focus on who I am. I am a daughter of Christ! I am a happily married woman. I am a mom of three beautiful kids. I want them to be proud of me and see what it means to stand for something when they look at my life.

When you take a stand for something, you open up the door for scrutiny. Being a celebrity tends to magnify that, but I don't want to be the poster child for a dress code. Instead, I'd love to help open dialogue about clothing ourselves in the things that truly matter. I want to use the platform God has given me to point women toward a different kind of wardrobe.

Colossians 3:12 says it this way, "Therefore, God's chosen ones, holy and loved, put on heartfelt compassion, kindness, humility, gentleness, and patience."

The best accessories aren't the clothes in my closet or the jewelry in my dresser. Instead, I want to showcase the qualities of Christ. When people look at me, I hope they see compassion, kindness, humility, gentleness, and patience.

How about you? When people look at you, what do you hope they see? Beyond just your hair and face and makeup, what's your image? What makes you, you? Why not take a minute to think about your image right now. (Don't worry. I'm not going anywhere.) In the space below write out the qualities you hope other people see in you.

A Pretty Heart

One of my favorite stories in the Bible is found in 1 Samuel 16. The prophet Samuel is given the task of choosing a new king for Israel. He knows the king will come from the household of Jesse, so Samuel makes the trek to Jesse's house. When he tells Jesse he is there to anoint the next king, Jesse parades his sons in front of Samuel, starting with the oldest. Jesse's sons are big and strong and impressive, but Samuel senses that none of them are to be chosen as king. In the middle of that story, we find a gem that shows where God's really looking when He looks at us.

"But the LORD said to Samuel, 'Do not look at his appearance or his stature, because I have rejected him. *Man does not see what the LORD sees, for man sees what is visible, but the LORD sees the heart*'" (1 Sam. 16:7, emphasis mine).

Jesse ended up parading seven of his sons in front of Samuel. But God rejected every single one of them. Why? Because God wasn't looking for the biggest and tallest son to be king. He didn't need someone extra handsome or extra rugged. God wanted someone with a heart like His. Here's a snapshot of how Samuel finally found him.

Samuel: Is this everybody?

Jesse: Well . . . actually there is one more. He's the baby of the family. I'm sure he's not king material, so I told him to stick with the sheep.

Samuel: I'll decide who's king material. Go and get him.

"So Jesse sent for him. He had beautiful eyes and a healthy, handsome appearance. Then the LORD said, 'Anoint him, for he is the one'" (v. 12).

That handsome boy was David and he would go on to be one of the greatest kings in Israel's history. He wrote much of the book of Psalms and turned the hearts of the entire nation toward God. Sure, he was handsome, but it wasn't his external appearance that impressed God. In 1 Samuel 13:14 God describes David as a "man according to His heart."

Society may have been looking for a big and tall king, a strong king or an intimidating king. But God wasn't looking at external stuff. God peeked into the inside and chose a king who would show off the things of God.

Sure, what we wear matters, but I didn't speak up about modesty on *DWTS* because I wanted to stick to some list of fashion rules that "they" consider modest. (Who are "they" anyway?) I wasn't interested in sparking a conversation about external stuff. I get that that's where our culture tends to focus. I live in a world that seems to be all about external appearances. But that's not where the Lord is looking for my beauty. He looks at my heart. I wanted to portray a modest heart, one clothed in the qualities of God like humility, righteousness, holiness, and strength. A heart filled with that kind of good stuff that can't help but ooze out from the inside to the outside.

As I look back on my *DWTS* journey, I hope that I sparked a conversation about something bigger than midriffs and hemlines. My specific convictions in those areas might not be your convictions, but they are true to my understanding of God's heart for modesty. They do fit through the filter of what my husband thinks is okay. And they are an external reflection of who I am on the inside.

Hide It Under a Bushel? No!

Erin's question at the end of the rumba was confirmation that the show's producers wanted me to be portrayed as a woman of faith. For each pre-show video package the producers cut hundreds of hours of footage, during many of which I didn't talk about my faith at all. But I think the producers realized early on how much my Christian walk related to some of the audience so they chose to piece together a storyline that in some way related to my faith and my family.

It wasn't my mission to go on *DWTS* and launch a conversation about modesty. Just like it wasn't necessarily my mission to go on the show and talk about my faith. It was always my mission to be true to who I am. It wasn't my primary goal to share Jesus Christ with the world, but that's a big part of who I am. It's natural that I would want to talk about it. Likewise, being a happily married woman committed to saving parts of myself for my husband is who I am. It's natural that I would want to talk about that too.

It reminds me of that old song you might have sung in Sunday school about our "light."

"Hide it under a bushel? No! I'm gonna let it shine!"

That sweet little children's song actually comes from a sermon that Jesus preached.

> "You are the salt of the earth. . . . You are the light of the world. A city situated on a hill cannot be hidden. No one lights a lamp and puts it under a basket, but rather on a lampstand, and it gives light for all who are in the house. In the same way, let your light shine before men, so that they may see your good works and give glory to your Father in heaven." (Matt. 5:13–16)

I want to shine like a bright light for Jesus in all areas of my life. I am so grateful to have been given the opportunity to shine for Jesus on the giant platform that came with *DWTS*, but I also want to shine for Him when it's just my family and me at home.

Sometimes, we tend to overromanticize being salt and light. Jesus was clear that not everyone would get it when we used our lives to point the spotlight toward Him. That was part of my experience too. Some people accused me of being "too Christian" or criticized me for "pushing my religion." Looking back, it's clear to me that I wasn't shoving, I was shining! Standing with conviction and shining the spotlight on Jesus won't always be met with a standing ovation, but we should do it anyway! Jesus has changed me from the inside out. I can't help but point others toward Him.

Hide it under a bushel? No way! I'm gonna let it shine. The next round of competition would offer the chance for me to shine brighter than ever before!

Chapter 4

A Clean. Slate·

"Do not grieve, because the joy of
the LORD is your stronghold."
—NEHEMIAH 8:10

Do you have a most memorable year?

Mine is 1995. It was the year we first gained access to the World Wide Web. (What did we ever do without it?) It was the year eBay was founded, right in my home state of California! And do you remember when we had to rewind movies after watching them on VCRs? Well, 1995 changed all of that thanks to the release of the DVD. That was good news because it was also the year we all first fell in love with Woody and the gang from *Toy Story*. (No rewinding required!) But for me, 1995 was so significant because it was filled with life-altering changes.

In my third week of *DWTS* competition, the contestants were asked to highlight our most memorable year. I chose 1995 because it was the year that *Full House* ended and Val proposed. It was a transition that moved me away from childhood and into adulthood. I went from one family, my *Full House* family, to my new family with Val as my husband. I was thrilled to share my memories from that year with the millions of fans who were watching the show.

Maybe it's because 1995 was such an important and exciting year for me. Maybe I was simply finding my stride in figuring out how to use this opportunity to shine. Either way, week three was one of my favorite weeks on the show.

As I headed into rehearsals, I had a high under my belt from the first show, when I impressed the judges with my secret contemporary dance skills! I also had a low under my belt from falling short being a fish out of water too quick in week two with my rumba. While I did feel a little whiplash from those two extreme reactions, I also felt like I could move forward on more even ground. I considered it a clean slate and decided it was time to let go of expectations and the pressure I was feeling as a result. I'm not sure I realized the full weight of that pressure. Once I set those burdens down I had a lot more bounce in my step. I finally felt free to enjoy the ride.

A *Full House* Tribute

My life was dramatically impacted by my role as D.J. Tanner on *Full House*. In addition to launching me toward the bright lights of stardom and locking in my passion for acting, *Full House* introduced me to some of the most important people in my world. The cast of the show truly became my second family.

As I thought about how to showcase my most memorable year, I knew I wanted to pay tribute to *Full House*. I couldn't think of a better way to do that than dancing to an Elvis song. Elvis was almost his own character on *Full House* with John Stamos always acting like Elvis and having Elvis impersonators on the show. Elvis was such a strong presence on our show he almost deserved his own dressing room! So, Mark and I decided to celebrate my most memorable year by dancing to "Blue Suede Shoes." As if that wasn't fun enough, we were assigned the jive—an upbeat, fast-paced dance that was a great fit for my personality.

Reliving such a pivotal year while learning a happy dance was fun enough, but the experience was made even sweeter by the support I received from my former *Full House* castmates Lori Loughlin and Andrea Barber. You might know them best as Aunt Becky and best friend Kimmy Gibbler. They made a special trip to the rehearsal studio to support and encourage me. Andrea and Scott Weinger, who played my boyfriend Steve on the show, were also in the audience for the live show that week. They joined with John Stamos, Dave Coulier, and Bob Saget (a.k.a. Uncle Jesse, Joey, and Danny Tanner) in rallying for votes through social media. They couldn't all make it to the set, but all of the cast members were extremely supportive. It was exciting to show the world that even after all these years, we are still such a huge part of each other's lives. Their cheers joined the chorus coming from my family and friends and fed into the excitement and joy I was feeling at this point in the journey.

I needed all of that love and support to carry me through the physical side of learning a jive. The jive is supposed to be lively and uninhibited. Cue: "Dancing Queen" music . . . "You can dance, you can jive, having the time of your life; ooh, see that girl, watch that scene, diggin' the dancing queen!" I bet at least your toes were tapping as you thought of that song. The jive makes everyone want to move! It is a dance that is really fun to watch and do, but it's very physically demanding. It's fast and involves a lot of hopping up and down. Rehearsals made me feel like I was in a cardio exercise class for hours! To top it off, this was the week of competition when our practice times were lengthened from four to six hours. We literally clocked in and clocked out for each rehearsal. We were not allowed to stay longer than our allotted time and were not permitted to rehearse off site. Our contracts made it clear that any couples that violated these rules would be instantly kicked off the show. Betcha didn't know dancing could be such serious business!

The length of our dance also increased by fifteen seconds this week. In real life, fifteen seconds feels like nothing. I can't even answer an e-mail in that amount of time! But as I was listening to "Blue Suede Shoes" for the first time in rehearsals, I could sense the difference that fifteen seconds could make in the dance world. I could almost feel how many more steps I was going to have to take. It made my body hurt just thinking about it! As we rehearsed, I learned just how precious and taxing fifteen seconds could be.

Attitude Is Everything

While I was determined to enjoy myself, that didn't always happen naturally. I picked up the steps to the jive very easily to Mark's surprise, but when I tried to merge those steps into a fluid routine adding choreographed arm movements, I just couldn't seem to do it. I was so frustrated! It was obvious to me that I wasn't dancing at the pace I wanted to be and that bothered me.

Remember how I told you that Mark was a very patient instructor? That's true! In general, his approach with me was gentle and I responded well to that. But a good coach also knows when to push his student, and this week Mark pushed me to respond differently to the challenges I was facing. To put it bluntly, he called me out on my bad attitude.

He said, "Your attitude is everything, so that's coming across in your movements and how you're dancing."

Mark warned me, "As soon as the song starts I can already see in your body language and in your face that you're not going to get through this routine."

He pointed out that the reason I did so well in week one was that I enjoyed myself. He knew from experience that the mental game is what starts separating the pack of contestants on *DWTS*. People who start getting mentally frustrated will get eliminated because the pressure will ultimately accompany them onto the dance floor. I didn't want my frustrations to lead to elimination. I knew I had to find a way to shake it off.

Mark approached me like a parent would approach a child who was letting their circumstances get the best of them. He told me to take a fifteen-minute break, breathe deep, and come back with a different attitude. None of that made it past the editing floor as the producers told our story for the show. This is the behind-the-scenes scoop you didn't see if you were watching us live. But it was such an important part of the process for me. I learned lessons in that rehearsal studio that changed how I want to respond in my life moving forward.

Because attitude really is everything.

Philippians 2:5 says it this way, "Make your own attitude that of Christ Jesus."

If we keep reading that passage, we see that's a tall order!

Who, existing in the form of God, did not consider equality with God as something to be used for His own advantage. Instead He emptied Himself by assuming the form of a slave, taking on the likeness of men. And when He had come as a man in His external form, He humbled Himself by becoming obedient to the point of death—even to death on a cross. (Phil. 2:6–8)

Jesus' attitude was humble and sacrificial. He chose to respond to His circumstances with love, patience, and gentleness. I won't do it perfectly, but I want to live like the Bible calls me to and choose an attitude that mirrors Christ's.

But how?

When we are frustrated or discouraged or sad or anxious, how do we respond like Jesus did? Sometimes we just have to choose it.

My son Lev is a fact machine. He's always sharing nuggets of information. Maybe he will win big on a trivia show someday! One of his favorite details he's shared with me is that it's a scientific fact that if you can force a smile, you can't help but have an attitude change. He's right! Did you know that researchers have found that smiling, especially when it's a big smile that travels all the way up to our eyes, produces a change in brain activity that corresponds with a happier mood? Even if you're faking it in the moment, if you can get the corners of your mouth to turn up and your eyes to light up, your brain will go into happy mode. Researchers have also found that people who smile have lower heart rates after completing a stressful task compared to those with a neutral or negative expression. No doubt, competing on the show was stressful at times, but I could help manage my body's response simply by choosing to smile through the journey. On the flipside, frowns have been shown to increase the body's stress response.[3] Attitude really is everything!

Researchers haven't just discovered that smiles impact the face they are planted on. Their effect is contagious! If one person sees another person smiling, mirror neurons will light up in the watcher's brain as if he is smiling himself. We can positively impact the attitudes of others just by flashing our pearly whites.[4]

Not being able to get the hang of the jive was one of those moments when I simply didn't feel like smiling. I was frustrated with myself but I knew, thanks to Mark's coaching and Lev's factoids, that if I could force a smile, it would change my attitude. So, I stepped off the dance floor for a break. I took a few deep breaths and asked the Lord to change my attitude. I envisioned my parents when they are dancing, and I determined to have as much fun as I've seen them have.

You know what? It worked!

There was a noticeable change right away. I stepped back on the dance floor and we went through the routine again. I sure felt different as I danced! Even the producers noticed. They didn't typically offer commentary, but the next time we worked through the routine they said they saw a night-and-day difference. My smile had flipped the switch! Mark said, "That's what I'm talking about. You changed your attitude and it changed everything."

That's a lesson that goes way beyond the dance floor. When I am frustrated with my kids, a smile has the power to diffuse the situation and remind me of how much fun they are. In my marriage, simply smiling at my husband will cause neurons to light up in his brain that will lead to lower stress and increased happiness. As I interact with others through work, church, and friendship, my attitude will impact the quality of those relationships.

My circumstances may not always be happy, but I can still choose to respond with joy. In fact, that was something I heard over and over from people who watched the show. They said:

- "Thank you for being joyful."
- "Thanks for responding with joy even when the judges were being critical."
- "I could see joy all over your face."

Choosing joy is God's idea! It's a theme woven throughout His Word.

- Galatians 5:22 lists joy as the fruit of the Spirit. It is what hangs from our lives because of Jesus.
- 1 Chronicles 16:33 says that God made even the trees of the forest to sing for joy. Ever seen a beautiful tree swaying in the breeze? That's joy on display!
- Esther 8:16 says that God's people have light and joy and gladness and honor. Joy is one of the hallmarks of believers.
- In Psalm 5:11 and Psalm 68:3 God commands us to be joyful.
- 2 Corinthians 7:4 says we can be overflowing with joy even in times of affliction.

Joy isn't the same as happiness. Happiness is totally dependent on external circumstances. If things go well, we are happy. If things don't go well, those happy feelings end.

Joy comes from something deeper and more significant. It is not dependent on circumstances, but is a consistent, unsinkable response to what Christ has done for us, instead of what is currently happening to us.

My friend, and one of my favorite Bible teachers, Angela Thomas said it this way, "JOY defined—the inner attitude of rejoicing in one's situation regardless of outward circumstances. One of the fruits of a right relationship with God."[5] (Angela is so wise! You'll read more from her later.)

Whew! That's good stuff, but it can also be a hard truth to wrestle with. Joy is the right response because of what God has done for us. Difficult circumstances cannot erase His love for us. Tough times cannot change what He has done for us. So, no matter what we face, we always have cause for joy. But joy also works like a barometer for the state of my heart. If I'm joy deficient, my focus is off.

When talking about joy, Angela went on to say, "The followers of Jesus have been given lavish gifts from God. Most of us open the ones we need most and too many of us leave the gift of joy unwrapped or still in the box."[6]

As I struggled to learn the jive, I could have chosen to stay frustrated. It would have compounded the problem, making learning more difficult, and it would have been like leaving a gift that God intended for me to have for this journey unwrapped on the ballroom floor.

The Superhero Power of Joy

First Chronicles 16:27 is describing God and says, "Splendor and majesty are before Him; strength and joy are in His place."

Psalm 16:11 became one of the verses I clung to during my *DWTS* journey. It says, "You reveal the path of life to me; *in Your presence is abundant joy*; in Your right hand are eternal pleasures" (emphasis mine).

Wherever God is, there is strength and joy but these are not qualities God keeps to Himself. Where God is, joy is. When we are in close proximity to Him, seeking to know Him, we will experience joy.

Why is joy such a gift? Is it just about warm fuzzies? No way! What's amazing about joy is that it works like a superhero power to strengthen us in times of weakness.

There's an Old Testament story in which the prophet Nehemiah is talking to God's people at a time when they are deeply troubled. The whole nation is weeping when Nehemiah says these words, "Go and eat what is rich, drink what is sweet, and send portions to those who have nothing prepared, since today is holy to our Lord. *Do not grieve, because the joy of the LORD is your stronghold*" (Neh. 8:10, emphasis mine).

Where can we find the strength to keep going when life is tough? Joy! When we feel weak, what gives us strength to carry on? Joy! Joy and strength are two sides of the same coin. Joy fortifies. It shores up. Sometimes it's the reinforcement we need to stay standing.

As Christians it's okay to let loose and have joy instead of getting overly wrapped up in our circumstances. My circumstances didn't change. The jive was still a difficult dance to learn. I was still feeling the pressure of competing on a live show watched by millions. I was still an amateur dancer trying to compete with Olympic athletes. Getting upset wasn't going to make any of that any easier but choosing joy did!

I was strengthened for the journey by making a conscious effort to be joyful along the way.

That may not always look like forcing a smile while learning a new dance routine. My sister noticed my decision to be joyful while on the show. She's a great mom who homeschools her four kids. She loves it! She's naturally joyful, but she told me that when she watched me perform and respond with joy on the show she recognized that sometimes she forgets to have fun. She took it as a reminder to put a smile on her face that would serve as an example of joy to her family and all those around her.

Whether you're a celebrity on a dancing competition or a homeschooling mom of four, attitude is everything. We may not be able to choose our circumstances, but we can choose to smile. We can choose joy.

In fact, my prayer is that Psalm 32:11 becomes the battle cry of the stressed out, worn out, frustrated, discouraged, and maxed out among us.

> Be glad in the LORD and rejoice,
> you righteous ones;
> shout for joy,
> all you upright in heart.

No matter what we face, we can force those happy brain neurons to keep firing by choosing to unwrap God's gift of joy.

A Joyful Jive

I don't mean to give the impression that we can choose joy once and for all. I didn't slap a smile on my face in rehearsals and then never feel another moment of stress for the duration of the show. Nope, stress and anxiety and nerves came in waves. Every time the waves hit, I had the choice to choose joy or to choose an attitude that would be less constructive.

The moment before we went live for week three was one of the moments I felt pummeled by nerves. The jive was a difficult dance to master with its sharp kicks and flicks, and there was one piece of choreography in the middle of the routine that was hit or miss with my steps. I wasn't consistently nailing it and I knew my nerves were getting to me even more because of it. I wasn't sure I was ready to showcase it in front of the watching world.

The stress must have shown on my face because right as we were standing on the dance floor, with the audience surrounding us, waiting for the video package to play before immediately going into the routine, Mark grabbed me and prayed with me. He took my hands, pulled them in close, and recited the Lord's Prayer, whispering it into my ear. Tears filled my eyes and a huge smile was upon my face as we both said, "Amen." It was a significant moment for me! Not only did I feel totally loved and supported by Mark, but it was also a huge answer to my prayers. One of my friends had been encouraging me to pray with Mark. My response was, "I'm praying about praying with Mark." I know that sounds silly, especially because I'm a praying gal and I'm rarely shy about it. I was certainly open to praying with Mark and wanted to, but I recognized the amount of time we'd be spending together day in and day out over what could potentially be several months so I hesitated initiating prayer because I didn't want to force it if it made him feel uncomfortable and make our time together awkward.

There's a difference between in-your-face and Spirit-led Christianity. I hadn't hid my faith from my partner or shied away from spiritual conversations at any point in the journey, but I wanted to personally pray with Mark when I felt it was the right time for the right reasons. When he initiated prayer and prayed for me, it was a very special moment and one I'll never forget. And, it was just the push I needed to let go of my fears and jive my heart out!

What Will You Choose?

Are you in a season of stretching and learning something new and stumbling a bit along the way? Can you not seem to master the "steps" of your roles at home or at work? Are you running a marathon without energy? Wondering how you will ever cross the finish line coasting on fumes?

I get it! I've been there. My time on *DWTS* was an opportunity for me to sharpen the tools in my arsenal that I need to live a full life off set. I was reminded that no matter what I face or how frustrated I am tempted to feel, I can choose to focus on Christ and in His presence there is fullness of joy.

What about you? Does your attitude stink? Are you compounding difficult circumstances by responding negatively?

If so, let me be the coach for a minute. Take a break. Breathe deep. Pray. Ask God to help you have an attitude more like His. Flash a smile. Hold it until those happy neurons start firing. Remember where your strength comes from. Have fun. And repeat this battle cry with me . . .

Be glad in the LORD and rejoice,
you righteous ones;
shout for joy,
all you upright in heart. (Ps. 32:11)

Chapter 5

All Grace
and No Truth

For the Lord disciplines the one He loves
and punishes every son He receives.
—HEBREWS 12:6

Imagine this.

It's a hectic Monday morning. I need to get the kids off to school and Val and I off to work. Between the laundry, the backpacks, the lunches, the scheduling, and the carpooling, there is too much to do and too little of me to go around. So, I do what all mamas must—I delegate! I tell Maks, my youngest, that he is in charge of breakfast for the whole family. If you know a preteen boy, you might be able to predict how this could turn out. We all sit down to the breakfast table to find that Maks has prepared us a feast that includes waffles, ice cream sundaes, French fries, Hot Pockets, Reese's peanut butter cups, and Doritos. With root beer floats to wash it down, of course! The totality of Maks's culinary expertise is on display. There's no time for me to whip up a healthier breakfast, so we all dig in. Truth be told, we all pig out. Then we push back from the table and head into our week with bellies full of sugar, carbs, and a side of grease.

If you know much about me, you know that this is a highly unlikely scenario. We have a family commitment to healthy eating and living, not because we are trying to follow the latest food fad, but because we recognize that our bodies are the vehicles we use to live our lives. If we fill them with junk, we are very likely to crash and burn.

In *Reshaping It All* I wrote about my food mantra this way,

> I love food. I love the smell, I love the taste, I love the variety. But I think we all have to come to terms with the fact that, first and foremost, food is fuel for our bodies. Let's get the entertainment aspect out of our heads for a minute and realize that it doesn't have to be a 24-7 buffet.[7]

Food is fuel. If the Bures filled our bodies with junk and tried to head into a busy week, we'd find that we didn't have the energy needed to focus and accomplish everything on our to-do list. While Maks's buffet might taste good for a moment, it wouldn't translate into the right kind of fuel we need to get the job done.

Over the years, my life and body have been transformed by coming to terms with this simple principle—garbage in, garbage out. If you're a computer programmer, you may recognize that phrase (often abbreviated as GIGO, for you techies). I don't speak geek, even though I live in the state that hosts Silicon Valley, geek mecca. But I'm a big believer in the GIGO principle. What I put into my body is what I can expect to get out. Put junk in. Get junk out. The same is true for the rest of my life. What I put into my mind is exactly what I get out. Where I invest my energy is where I can expect to get results.

What does that have to do with my time on *Dancing with the Stars*? Everything! Week four was switch-up week. Just when we were all starting to get comfortable, America voted to switch the teams, partnering each celebrity with a different dance professional. If I had to describe that week as a food, I might choose the imaginary breakfast buffet that Maks prepared. It was one of the most enjoyable weeks of the entire competition. Just like sitting down to a giant hot fudge sundae with my family, everything about that week went down smooth, but ultimately it was a week marked by all grace and no truth, resulting in scores that tied the very low scores I received for the rumba. That landed me at the bottom of the leader board with 28 out of 40 points, leaving me way behind all the other contestants.

Week Four, and the Livin' Is Easy

I knew that switch-up week was coming, and I was most hoping to be partnered with Val or Derek. Maks, who really is a big teddy bear underneath it all, felt too intimidating, and I was hesitant to be paired with Tony Dovolani. For the bulk of the show, Tony was partnered with Nene Leakes. You might know Nene best for her role in the *Real Housewives of Atlanta*. I'd watched Tony and Nene own it on the dance floor during every round of the competition, and I knew Tony was an accomplished dancer and fabulous instructor, but he also liked to joke at my expense. He knew my tendency to think more conservatively and loved to hone in on that to make me squirm. It was all in good fun but he was always out to make me blush! Because of that, I was hoping he would not be my new partner for switch-up week. But when the door flung open to reveal my new partner while the cameras rolled, there stood Tony.

As we talked through our initial reactions about our new partnership, he compared how different it was going to be for him to have had someone like Nene, known for her unfiltered and unabashed dominant personality, to someone like me, who was much more reserved and blushed at a moment's notice; not to mention our height difference with Nene standing tall at 5'10" and me at 5'2". But Tony quickly put my fears to rest. As we settled in to our new roles of teacher and student, Tony was very sweet and professional. He put up a boundary and traded in the silly jokes for serious but gentle instruction, which was a great relief.

We were assigned the quickstep and given the song "Ballroom Blitz" to dance to. This was technically my first ballroom dance of the show. To understand why, let me give you a crash course in ballroom dance terminology. (You didn't know that you'd enrolled in Ballroom Dance for Dummies when you bought this book, did you?) There are five points of connection in a ballroom

Quickstep: True to its name, the quickstep is a dance characterized by quick steps set to fast-paced music. It's intended to be a dance that is very energetic, yet elegant. Quickstep dancers are supposed to maintain very straight upper-body posture while appearing very light on their feet.

frame. If you have ballroom dancing aspirations of your own or just love quirky trivia like my guy, Lev, check out the five points of connection on the next page. The dances I'd performed in previous weeks didn't require me to be in a frame with the five points of connection, so they weren't technically ballroom dances. (But that didn't make them any easier!)

I had a blast learning with Tony. He was such a good teacher and I was totally at ease. During that week I never forgot my choreography. I felt no pressure at all. Even though we were still training for six hours a day and looking ahead to a live performance in front of millions, Tony managed to make it feel light and breezy. It was like I was on a ballroom dance cruise, not a dance competition. Others noticed a difference in me too. They pointed out that I seemed more relaxed and that my smile was bigger and brighter.

But that's not all they noticed. At one point Mark popped into our room during rehearsal. It was a pattern of mine that any time someone poked their head into the studio while I was dancing, it threw me. Having unexpected visitors rattled me because my nerves were already on high alert. So, when Mark stopped by unannounced to watch us dance, I was bothered by the interruption. (Particularly because Mark was invited to watch our dance the day before by Tony but refused the invitation and said he wanted it to be a surprise at dress rehearsal.) Obviously, Mark had seen me dance before. He had been training me for weeks. He also knew having someone else in the room unexpectedly rattled my nerves. And with him being my long-term coach, I naturally felt more pressure to do a good job with my new partner in front of him. The combination suddenly filled the room with tension and I didn't want to dance in front of Mark. Mark kept digging a bit, telling me I was acting like a baby and maybe

Five Points of Ballroom Connection.

Just in case you ever find yourself in a ballroom dancing competition, or just want to wow your friends at a wedding reception, here is a crash course in the five points of connection in ballroom dance.

Connection Point #1: Hand to Hand

The gentleman's left hand meets the lady's right hand. The lady places her hand on top of the man's hand and her thumb under his thumb. Palms are closed together.

Connection Point #2: Wrist to Underarm

Often called the "forgotten point of contact," this requires the man's inside wrist to be in an upright position. His fingers and thumb are held together and his palm is angled toward his own body. The lady places her left underarm on top of the man's wrist to create the second point of connection.

Connection Point #3: Hand to Shoulder

Once a man's wrist is in position, he lays his closed right hand onto his partner's left shoulder blade.

Connection Point #4: Hand to Arm

The lady takes her left hand and places it on the man's upper right arm. With her thumb and middle finger she holds a light grip on his upper arm.

Connection Point #5: Shoulder to Chest

The fifth point of connection is reserved for intermediate dancers because it is difficult to master. It requires the lady to align her right shoulder to the center of the man's chest. Then the man's right shoulder is lined up with the center on the lady's chest. This results in an off-center position.[8]

I was, but suddenly I felt like my ship docked and my cruise was coming to an end. Tony stepped in and kicked everyone out of the room, and immediately redirected our conversation and focused on happy things, and the chill mood I had come to love about working with Tony returned.

Because I really was interested in Mark's feedback, we scheduled a time for him to come back and see the dance. I was prepared for his critique so I wasn't rattled. He didn't say anything to me immediately, but later he pulled me aside and said, "Your frame is terrible. You're going to get marked off for that." He recruited another female dancer to model good form for me and sent me back into the rehearsal studio.

As the week progressed, I asked Tony a couple of times if my form was okay. He was always encouraging, saying things like, "Don't worry about it," "You're great," "Just relax," and "You're gonna kill it."

I killed something all right, but it wasn't the dance. It was my scores! I ended up with 7s across the board. Tony and I had a blast on the dance floor but when we got to the judges, they saw what Mark had seen during rehearsals. They pointed out that I missed two of the five points of connection. It was the kind of framework they would have expected to see in round one or two of the competition, and something they sympathized with because it was the first time dancing with Tony, but at this stage of the game, it wasn't enough and I watched my name plummet to the bottom of the leader board.

Those scores were not a commentary on Tony's abilities as a dancer or an instructor. He's among the most accomplished dancers in the world. He's been on *DWTS* since the second season, coaching celebrities and securing a mirrorball trophy of his own. But his style (as much as I loved it) wasn't what I needed. Maybe it was because it was switch-up week and Tony wanted nothing but enjoyment for me, but what I needed in the competition was to be challenged. I needed to be pushed. Switch-up week was one of the most comfortable weeks I experienced on the show, but ultimately it resulted in a weaker performance. We all love to be comfortable. We all want to have fun, but this week was a jolting reminder that just because something is comfortable and feels good, that doesn't mean that's what's best for us.

All Grace and No Truth

Like every other leg of my *DWTS* journey, switch-up week proved to be a parallel to my Christian faith. The truth in God's Word isn't always easy to digest. It doesn't always feel good to live like He's called us to live. Sometimes we feel beat up and bruised as we seek to swim upstream against the culture and live out His plan, but He stretches us in ways that are ultimately for our good.

Yes, He is a God of grace. But He is also a God of truth.

In fact, truth is one of the words Jesus used to describe Himself during His time on the earth.

In John 14:6 Jesus was teaching His disciples when He said, "I am the way, the truth, and the life. No one comes to the Father except through Me."

Jesus isn't *a* truth or *my* truth. He is *the* truth. I can take His teachings to the bank!

In John 8:31–32 we read, "So Jesus said to the Jews who had believed Him, 'If you continue in My word, you really are My disciples. You will know the truth, and the truth will set you free.'"

We live in a culture that says that relative truth is the path to freedom. If we just let everyone decide for themselves what truth is, then we're in the sweet spot. The Bible takes a very different stance. Admittedly, it can be a tough pill to swallow. God is truth. His Word is truth. That doesn't mean it's always easy to hear and apply what He wants us to do. Living the way God calls us to is often tough! But knowing the truth of who God is and how He calls us to live, ultimately leads to our freedom.

The idea that absolute truth is the key to our freedom seems counterintuitive. Maybe if we circle back to my food analogy, we can get a better grasp on it. During the early years of my marriage, I coped with all of the changes that came with getting married—pulling the brakes on my acting career and relocating from California to Canada (brrr!)—by eating. More specifically, I ate whatever I wanted, whenever I wanted. Ice cream late at night? Sure! Cookies for breakfast? Why not!

When it came to food, I was suddenly uninhibited. I threw the "rules" for healthy eating totally out the window and used food to help me cope with a tidal wave of transitions. But I didn't find freedom. Instead, I ended up in bondage to an eating disorder. True freedom came when I learned to respect the "rules" of my body and follow them and ditched my "anything goes" approach to food.

Just like taking an indulgent approach to food led to an unhealthy body, if I focus on God's graceful side and ignore the truth of His Word, the result is an anemic faith that doesn't give me the strength I need to really live my life for Him.

That pattern extends to how we treat each other. We need people in our lives who will push us out of our comfort zones. We need people who will lovingly point out sin. We need coaches in our corner who will push us to be better than we are.

Here's an example of what that looks like in my life.

Post *DWTS*, in the fall when school started, I knew my fall and winter were going to get really busy. I was scheduled to do three films for the Hallmark Channel back-to-back, all of which were being filmed out of town. My husband and kids have always been on board with me being away and filming for three-week stints at various times throughout the year, but because *DWTS* made the start of the year unusually grueling, my daughter in particular needed to share her heart with me. It was a heavy dose of truth. And it hurt!

After coming home from Utah, having filmed my first of the three movies, *Christmas Under Wraps*, my daughter wasn't exactly happy when I arrived. I couldn't quite figure out why I was getting the cold shoulder, since we'd been talking, face-timing, and texting the entire time I was gone. Turned out, she missed me. And her way of showing me was by being mad at me. If anyone has a manual on figuring out the emotions of teenage girls, please send it to my address! Val was put in the middle being the go-between for a few days when he finally said, "Honey, you need to sit down and talk with Natasha. She has some things to tell you, and it needs to be a face-to-face conversation. She told me what's going on and she's ready to tell you." Great! I was ready to talk the day I got home and was ready to share a piece of my irritated mind at the unwelcoming homecoming I got from her. I picked up Natasha from school and took her out to a late lunch.

"What's going on?" I asked.

Truth be told, I had my mom speech all ready for her about how acting out and giving me the silent treatment wasn't respectful nor was it going to get her what she wanted.

I was prepared to talk and lecture her until her eyes couldn't roll back into her head any further, when she very earnestly and honestly started sharing with me how she felt.

"Mom, you weren't home much when you were on *DWTS*, and even though we loved it, I missed you. And now, you just left again for a movie, and you're leaving again in a month for another. I just don't feel like you do 'regular mom' stuff anymore. Papa always takes us to school. Papa picks us up. Papa makes our lunches. Since school started, you even stopped doing morning devotionals with us."

Ouch!

Sometimes truth feels like a punch in the gut! In this case, I wanted to hold up a glove to defend myself so I asked about all the things I do with Natasha and the boys and, particularly, about the summer that had just passed. I always choose not to work in June, July, and August so I can spend every moment with my kids. I felt she so easily dismissed those summer months to try to prove her point.

Luckily we were both able to lay the boxing gloves down and talk it through because we love each other. Natasha admitted that there were many things I did do with her and that the summer was great, but said that I was always multitasking while being with them. She didn't feel like she ever had my full attention. That stung my well-intentioned mom heart. Why? Because it was the truth!

What Natasha wanted most was my full devotion and attention whenever I was with her. My boys wanted the same thing. I can look back on my years as a mother and honestly say that I've given them that pretty consistently, but 2014 became a fruitful year in regard to work and it took me away from many motherhood tasks I've always done on a regular basis. While I am grateful for my work, and recognize it's necessity to help provide for my family (not to mention, I'm passionate about what I do!), I had to take a hard look at what my priorities had become.

As Natasha's words settled into my heart—and I'm not gonna lie, they hurt—I knew my priorities had become a little too much about me.

Natasha could have let those feelings continue to fester in her heart. She could have faked it and tried to pretend that everything was okay. She could have vented her frustrations to her friends and slapped on a happy face whenever we were together. I'm sure that conversation was as difficult for her as it was for me. But an all-grace-and-no-truth approach wouldn't have been better in the long run. Her silence would have driven a wedge between us and eventually the truth would have come out, likely in ways even more painful than our chat over lunch.

I was grateful Natasha told me the truth. It's easy to forget that sometimes sharing your feelings can be scary or difficult when you're sixteen years old. I was so grateful for her grace in allowing me to make some necessary changes to get my priorities back on track. It didn't mean I abandoned my work obligations or reneged on my contracts. It just meant that I made the things she talked about a priority again, like our family daily devotionals, putting away my cell phone or shutting down the computer when I was with them, driving them to and from school and practices as much as possible, and scheduling meetings when they were in school.

And guess what? God knows what He is talking about. The truth really did set us free! We were free to enjoy each other more as a family. Free to spend time together without distractions and free to connect without anger, resentment, and hurt coming between us.

Discipline Is Spelled L-O-V-E

In that conversation with Natasha, she was the one speaking truth and I was the one who needed a course correction. But usually the shoes are on the opposite feet! Every loving parent will tell you that discipline is a necessary part of the parent/child equation. A parent who is wishy-washy on discipline or refuses to acknowledge and correct their child's mistakes will end up with a tiny tyrant. It may not always feel like the most loving thing to do to discipline a child; after all, discipline is almost always painful for both parties. But in reality, consistent discipline is, in fact, a gift of love. The end result is discernment, self-control, and an allegiance to doing what's right. Those are qualities that will take your child a long way, and he will flush his life right down the toilet if he tries to make it without them.

That certainly doesn't mean that loving correction is an easy bull's-eye to hit! Natasha helped me learn this lesson too.

American Idol Mama

Natasha can sing. She discovered her voice and love for singing in the sixth grade, but it hasn't been until the last two years that she realized it was her God-given talent and passion. I encouraged Natasha to take singing lessons so she could learn to use her instrument to its fullest potential and discover all that it was capable of.

Recently, she'd been working on a very difficult song sung by a powerhouse singer. Natasha was eager to have me listen to her version of the song. She'd been practicing all week. As I did, I was so impressed by the strength of her voice and the clarity she sang with. I'd never heard her sing in this style and

I was one proud mama! But I also heard where notes were a bit weak in places and needed more work on control during transitions.

In the moment just before she finished singing, my thoughts quickly searched for the right response to her performance. She knows that I'm a big cheerleader and I love to whoop and holler when I'm excited and cheering someone on. And while I wanted to whoop and holler because she did such a fantastic job, I also didn't want to overdo it because I knew I needed to share some constructive criticism with her. I also didn't want to be a downer or seem unenthusiastic. I was completely torn in the moment between wanting to encourage (that's grace!) and needing to be honest that there was room for improvement (that's truth!). And if any of you reading this have a teenager, you're feeling my pain of how emotional and touchy this kind of thing can be! It can go south in a matter of seconds and then you're still feeling the effects for days.

But you don't have to be a teenager for criticism to launch you into meltdown mode. If I were to poll the readers of this book and ask, "Who loves to be disciplined?" I'd predict I would end up with a big ol' goose egg. Nobody likes their mistakes pointed out and corrected. When we think of the word *discipline*, we often picture the parent/child relationship, for good reason, but discipline can take on many forms. Maybe it looks like constructive criticism from a boss or friend. Maybe something goes haywire and you suddenly realize the need to course correct. Often discipline comes through the consequences of our wrong choices. It rarely feels good, but discipline is for our good. If you're not sure about that, picture that two-year-old throwing a stomping, screaming fit on the floor in Target. Left unchecked and undisciplined, that behavior is not going to result in a happy, well-adjusted child. (Or a happy, well-adjusted mama!)

The truth is that discipline is tied to love. I'd love to take the credit for that idea, but I can't. God came up with it first.

Hebrews 12:6 says, "For the Lord disciplines the one He loves and punishes every son He receives."

This is a picture of the beautiful balance between grace and truth. It's because of His grace toward us that He receives us as His children and because of His unswerving allegiance to truth that He disciplines us when we miss His mark. We like grace because it feels good, but grace with the absence of truth isn't what's best for us. It's because of this that God's Word encourages us to develop a love for discipline.

Proverbs 12:1 says, "Whoever loves discipline loves knowledge, but one who hates correction is stupid." Those words may seem harsh, but the reality is that when we hate discipline and avoid it at every turn, that will ultimately lead to our demise.

Natasha and I are still learning this lesson together. She finished singing and immediately looked to me for a reaction. She caught on to my confusion before a word came out of my mouth because her face dropped. Apparently I didn't whoo-hoo quickly enough and had a plastered smile on my face and she knew something was up. I tried to recover immediately by telling her how proud and impressed I was. I really was! She didn't totally believe me and started crying. I fessed up that I was trying to choose the right reaction that communicated that I thought it was amazing but there were still places that needed work and growth. I hugged her so tight and cried with her. I felt terrible. I was trying so hard not to blow that beautiful moment, but that's exactly what I did by overthinking it.

In that moment, I had empathy for every parent of an *American Idol* contestant whose audition went awry. You know the kind. They get up to sing in front of the judges with their paper number stuck to their shirt and within two seconds it's obvious that they can't carry a tune in a bucket. That doesn't stop them from singing their hearts out. Simon Cowell's eyes roll back in his head. One judge puts her fingers in her ears. They actually try to stop the audition part way through, but the contestant won't have it. They keep singing for all they're worth. When the train wreck is over, Randy Jackson declares, "That was a little pitchy, dog." Simon says something rude and insulting and the contestant runs out of the room, sobbing. That would be bad enough, but the tape still has to be played in front of millions of viewers and then talked about around water coolers and viewed in slow motion on YouTube.

All grace and no truth was the track that allowed the train wreck to happen. The more loving thing to do would have been for someone, anyone, to point out that the heartbroken contestant choose a different reality TV show or at least enroll in singing lessons before making their way onto the *American Idol* stage.

Natasha's song was nothing like an *American Idol* audition gone wrong. She really can sing! But I would not have been doing her any favors by pretending there was no room for improvement.

We talked it out and the tears stopped. Thankfully, she didn't stay disappointed because she knew that my honest criticism came from a place of love. Sometimes, I feel like I'm a little too constructive and critical, but as a parent, it's inevitable because I care. Truth in love. Sometimes you get a big whoop-whoop and sometimes you get tears. But in the end, there's always growth. And that's the goal.

S-T-R-E-T-C-H-E-D

Switch-up week was fun, but it was all giggles and no glory. The end result was a dance that missed the mark in the judges' eyes and the scores to prove it. I did learn some valuable lessons from Tony about how to enjoy the process and put my mind at ease more, which I was incredibly grateful for, but I also gained a new appreciation for Mark's teaching style and couldn't wait to return to the studio with him.

Ultimately, it was a picture for the way the Lord deals with me as His child. He's not overly permissive, allowing His children to do whatever they want, even if it results in their downfall. He is the plumb line of truth, and He will correct us when we are off course. But He's not a drill sergeant either, dishing out punishment in ways that are unnecessarily harsh.

Just like Mark pushed me during training to stretch me beyond what was comfortable, God pushes us to the point that we are uncomfortable often. But the motivation for His discipline is always love and the goal is always growth.

If we think of His discipline like a parent disciplining their child (because that's what it is), we find that He doesn't take either of the two extreme approaches.

> "But when the goodness of God and His love for mankind appeared, He saved us—not by works of righteousness that we had done, but according to His mercy, through the washing of regeneration and renewal by the Holy Spirit." (Titus 3:4–5)

He's not a dictator, just wanting to point His finger at every flaw and expecting me to fix it immediately. And there is no excessive permissiveness where He allows me to do whatever I want either. That's a good thing, because I don't want to be that toddler pitching a fit in Target! Ew!

God's discipline is the process of being stretched, with the goal of molding me to look more and more like Him. It doesn't always feel good. In fact, Hebrews 12:11 assures us that discipline will be painful at the time. But when we submit to it, it produces peace and righteousness in our lives. There are lots of times my flesh prefers the all-grace-and-no-truth approach to faith, but ultimately I'm grateful to serve the God of truth because His loving correction is pushing me toward greater freedom in Him. And when I look more like Him, I am better positioned to live out His truth in the world.

> For further study, be sure to check out the appendix section, where you'll find some guidelines on how to find a truth-centered church and my recommendations for Bible studies jam-packed with God's truth.

Chapter 6

Avoiding the Snare

The fear of man is a snare, but the one who
trusts in the LORD is protected.
—PROVERBS 29:25

Who knew you could do battle in a seashell bra and a mermaid skirt?

Week five of the competition was Disney week. Mark and I got our first-choice song "Under the Sea" sung by Sebastian to Ariel on why life was so much better below the waves. I had no idea that a light-hearted dance between a mermaid and a crab could create so much controversy and internal turmoil. It ended up being one of my biggest struggles in all the weeks of my *DWTS* experience and not because of the choreography.

> I was terribly sick this week and had to practice with a cold and fever.

Week five was the halfway point. I was finding my groove as a dancer and a competitor, but it turns out I still had a lot to learn about what it means to stand with conviction.

Mark and I were dancing the samba and I was going to be Ariel. I was giddy at first, since *The Little Mermaid* is my favorite Disney movie and Ariel is hands-down my favorite Disney princess. (No offense to Cinderella and Snow White, of course!) But as the details of the dance began to take shape, my emotions shifted from excited to nauseous. Mark approached me early on before we met with the costume department and said, "Have an open mind. Hear me out on this one . . . I'm Sebastian, dressed in all red like a crab, and you're Ariel, so I'm thinking really big seashells," as he cupped his hands over his chest, "and the mermaid skirt. Are you willing to show a little skin?"

> The samba is a medium-tempo dance typically performed to Latin music. Originally from Brazil, the samba is a high-energy dance characterized by lots of hip and foot movement.

Gulp! I'd already taken a stand for modesty at the start of the show and again in week two when Mark wanted to dance the rumba without a shirt. Those two comments had created a lot of buzz and I knew that people were watching me to see if I was going to follow through on my conservative commitments.

Before the Ariel costume was pitched, Mark and I had already decided not to talk about modesty any more in front of the cameras. It's not that I was backpedaling or flip-flopping on the issue. Modesty matters to God, and so it matters to me. But I had already clearly taken my stand. I didn't want to be known as the "modesty queen." I simply wanted to honor Christ in every way.

Remember how I said that I wanted to stay on the more modest side of *DWTS* costumes in week one? What I didn't say was that I wasn't going to show anything from my neck down to my ankles. In fact, I didn't give my definition of what "on the modest side" meant to *me*, which I do believe is relative. I intentionally left it open enough so that I could have leniency to wear the costumes I felt comfortable with while drawing from my own personal convictions. I was very careful about how I talked about the issue because I didn't want to dig a hole and get stuck in it, but this week I learned that others would dig that hole for you if you let them.

Weaving a Safety Net

Mark and I headed off to wardrobe to collaborate on costumes that captured the fun and frivolity of Ariel and Sebastian without making me uncomfortable. If you've seen *The Little Mermaid* (who hasn't?), you know that Ariel won't win any modesty awards. Her iconic look includes a teeny tiny purple seashell bra and a mermaid tail with a very deep V at the waistline. I don't have fins, so we knew we would have to represent Ariel's tail with some sort of skirt.

Mark knew I was uncomfortable showing certain areas of skin, so from the beginning he helped make adjustments. As the costumers sketched out the options, a wrestling match of sorts began in me. I knew what my personal convictions were. I knew I would never wear something that made me feel uncomfortable. I refused to be pressured into putting on something that just didn't feel right. I also knew that I was unwilling to disrespect my family, my husband and children, in any way by what I wore. Practically, that meant that I didn't want to show a lot of cleavage on stage. I also knew that I didn't want to copy Ariel's deep V under my belly button. These were easy fixes. The costumers sketched up a top and Mark said, "Get the biggest set of shells you can find!" They also removed the V from the top of the skirt and drew it so it hit in a straight line sitting just an inch below my bellybutton. But that still left a big hurdle to clear—my midriff.

I don't personally have a problem with midriff when it comes to fashion. Certainly, there are some lines of midriff that can be too exposed, but I come from L.A. Entertainment and fashion are a huge part of my culture. Maybe that's why I don't see a woman's midriff and automatically see it as immodest. And there was no way around it—if I was going to be Ariel, I was going to need to show a little tummy. But I was worried! I knew the standard had been set and I didn't want to compromise my testimony over something as trivial as a dance costume.

It was time to rally the troops! I knew that Val trusted me to make the right decision. I was confident that his primary concern would be my comfort, but I wanted a few other viewpoints from people whose opinion I value.

Proverbs 12:15 says it this way, "A fool's way is right in his own eyes, but whoever listens to counsel is wise." I didn't want to be foolish by making this decision all on my own. There is wisdom in listening to others.

Proverbs 11:14 says, "Without guidance, people fall, but with many counselors there is deliverance." God is clearly serious about this idea of seeking wise counsel. If we skip ahead a few chapters we read the same advice repeated. "For you should wage war with sound guidance—victory comes with many counselors" (Prov. 24:6).

If I was going to take this leap, I wanted some wise people as my safety net. If my costuming choices resulted in a war of public opinions, I wanted the victory that the Bible promises wise counsel can deliver, so I reached out to four important people in my life: my mom Barbara, my sister Melissa, the leader of my prayer teams, Clare, and a pastor-friend of mine, Brad.

I picked those four individuals because I knew that they were all solid in their commitment to and understanding of the Word of God. They were all people I knew would give me wise counsel. And they were all people who I knew would look out for my best interests. But I knew they could offer four different perspectives. I asked each one of them the same question, "Do you think this costume will compromise me?"

After sending out a request for prayer among my intimate group of praying friends, Clare responded without a hint of hesitation. She said, "Girl, go for it! It's Ariel. You're dancing. You're in a competition. If you're comfortable with it, wear it."

Whew! That felt good because she seemed to understand *why* I had decided I could wear the Ariel costume and not violate my personal boundaries.

This was a dance competition, so there was some wiggle room to wear something that I wouldn't normally wear in real life. Can't you just picture me showing up to my son's hockey practice in a dance costume? Oh, the eye rolls! But I also took into consideration the spirit of the song "Under the Sea." This was a fun song written with children in mind. I couldn't find anything in the Ariel costume that was being sexy for the sake of sex. If the Disney princesses were parading in lingerie, I'd have a problem with that. And so would lots of other parents! But every little girl loves the Disney princesses because they were created to entertain children. That's the heartbeat of Disney. It's supposed to be for children's enjoyment and amusement, not to showcase sexuality. All of that built to a level of comfort that helped me decide, "I can do this!"

My friend Brad, who is a pastor in the South, also encouraged me to go for it. Like many Southern pastors, Brad is pretty conservative, but even as a conservative pastor and a man, his point of view was that I could dress as Ariel and not compromise my testimony. He said, "Buddy, I'm so proud of you! For everything you've stood for and everything you've said. I trust that you are making the best decisions for yourself and I know your heart is to represent Christ in all that you do and you've proven that. So whatever your costume is, you go out there and represent Christ well!"

Clare and Brad's encouragement sure felt like the safety net God promises will come from seeking wise counsel, but that net started to tatter a bit when I heard back from my mom and sister.

My mom was torn. On the one hand she trusted me to make the right decision, but on the other hand she worried about public criticism.

My sister took a much harder stance. She pulled up pictures of Ariel on the Internet and said, "I'm sorry to say this, but yes, I think it compromises what you've stood for if you come out in this costume."

Ugh.

I knew my sister had my best interests in mind, but her hesitations muddied the waters in my heart. As we continued to dialogue about it, she made suggestions like covering my stomach with nude-colored fabric or wearing Ariel's wedding dress for the dance, but none of it seemed to work or fit with the song. After all, Ariel isn't wearing a wedding gown under the sea!

I wanted to go for it, but I couldn't seem to shake those words from my mom and sister. They are two of the most important women in my life, whose opinions I value greatly, and I was torn. In my heart a battle started raging.

Sea Sick!

Because of the intense time line of a live show, I had to make an immediate decision. Because I knew in my gut I could wear a modified Ariel costume and still stick to my convictions, I decided to go for it. As the seamstresses started building the costume, the head of the department assured me they could modify it along the way to fit my comfort level, but there was no going back. There was no time to develop a whole new costume concept from scratch if I didn't like this one. I was going out as Ariel, but I was literally sick to my stomach about it. I had so much anxiety about whether or not my testimony was going to be ruined by one wardrobe choice.

Looking back, I can see that all that anxiety was an unhealthy response. To be honest, as I'm writing this, I can actually feel the wave of nausea I felt at the time rise up in my stomach now because of how strong it was. But I didn't need to make myself sick over it. I realized I got off track in making the opinions of others my primary concern instead of focusing first and foremost on what would please the Lord.

Proverbs 29:25 should be standard issue armor for every Christian! It's one of those verses we need to survive: "The fear of man is a snare, but the one who trusts in the LORD is protected."

Fear of man is the worry that we won't measure up, that we will be criticized, that someone won't approve of the choices we are making. The Bible calls this a trap. Why? Because fear of man works like a chain that binds us to public opinion. Instead of living free, we are shackled by worry and fear of what someone else might think of us. The truth is, it's impossible to please everyone. If they look hard enough, people can always find something to be critical about. (Just check my Facebook page regularly and you'll see what I mean.) But safety is found in trusting God. He's not critical, but freely accepts us just as we are. Yes, He calls us to strive to live more and more like Him, but He's not watching from heaven, waiting for us to misstep so He can zap us with a lightning bolt! There is freedom and safety in living our lives for Him and intentionally turning down the volume on the chatter of the crowd.

In fact, turning down the volume helped the tide start to turn in my anxiety battle. During this week of competition, I stopped reading the comments on Facebook and Twitter. I simply had to turn it off. There were too many voices in my head: fans, family, Mark, the costumers, even my four counselors. I needed to be able to hear the two voices that mattered most, the Lord's and my own.

A Disney Princess Is Born!

Before I knew it, it was time for my first fitting.

I texted my mom and my sister and said, "I'm going in for my fitting. Will you please pray for me? I'm trying on this costume for the first time."

My mom's response gave me so much peace.

She wrote, "Honey, I keep praying about this for you, and what I keep hearing the Lord say to me is: Would you feel comfortable if Jesus were sitting in the audience watching you? If so, if there is no embarrassment or shame for you in any way wearing that costume, then you wear it and that's it. Don't think another thing about it."

Suddenly the crowd I had feared for days just melted away. Jesus was going to be in the audience when I danced as Ariel because He is always with me (Matt. 28:20). This wasn't between me and my sister. It wasn't between me and my Facebook followers. It wasn't between me and Christian bloggers. This was a decision best made between me and Jesus.

Fear of man had tripped me up and I wanted to be untethered! I needed to be reminded of my commitment to live for an audience of one. Once that switch had been flipped, I headed into my fitting with renewed confidence. I was pleasantly surprised by the designer's creation. The green scale-like material of the mermaid skirt was so realistic and beautiful and the purple seashells were as big and blingy as they promised me they'd be! To my surprise, they added three to four inches of beaded fringe to the bottom of the top and raised the waist of the skirt above my bellybutton all the way around so that between the two modifications most of my midriff was covered. I was filled with gratitude toward the costume department for working so hard to create something that made me feel as beautiful as Ariel and as confident as I needed to be.

My mood shifted from anxious back to excited. The costume was so much fun! There was nothing sexy about it. In fact, it was every little girl's childhood dream come true! I texted my mom and sister and said, "I feel like a Disney princess!" Praise God I felt great freedom and relief and felt no hesitation wearing it, knowing exactly who would be sitting in the audience.

Those emotions spilled out onto the dance floor because our "Under the Sea" routine received one 8 and three 9s. Donnie Osmond, who was guest judging that week, gave me the thumbs-up as I approached the judges' table and said, "Candace, I know that being at the bottom of the leaderboard (from last week) is very discouraging. Don't give up, because what I just saw was so promising. You were fantastic!" Carrie Ann went on to say, "You are one of my favorite movers on this season. I love watching you when you're in the zone and feeling comfortable. I relate to the way you move. It's so strong, so earthy, and so powerful. But you have another notch to you, and it's just a mind game, because you are incredible, Candace!" All the kind words from the judges made me feel proud, but mostly I was proud of myself for sticking to my personal convictions, even when it required me to swim upstream.

> To help calm my nerves and stay focused before performances, Mark and I did deep-breathing exercises. We also did push-ups and plank holds to get our bodies warm and sweating so we didn't go into the dance cold. FYI, I can out-plank Mark!

> Costumes can make you sweat! My Ariel costume weighed seven pounds and my silver-beaded jive dress weighed in at ten pounds!

The Fight after the Fight

I wish I could say that the fight over that mermaid costume ended when I exited the dance floor, but it didn't. While many people wrote to me saying that this was their favorite dance of the season, there were also people who criticized my choices. Most of the negative chatter happened online through social media. While it was no fun to be the guinea pig, I'm grateful for the exposure that this situation gave me because it gives me the opportunity to address a growing challenge in the modern church and gives me some authority to ask this question: As Christians, how should we treat each other online?

My Facebook ballooned to over 1 million followers during my time on *DWTS* and I gained somewhere in the neighborhood of half a million new Instagram and Twitter followers. I was obligated to post on social media as part of my *DWTS* experience, which I loved doing anyway, but the growth was so explosive that it took on a life of its own.

Because so many celebs have "people" who run their social media for them, the question begs, who does mine? I mean, who *actually* manages, posts, and comments on all my social media? I do! Not a personal assistant, not my publicist, not my agent or managers, not my kids (well, sometimes if they hack it), but me. Which means, I'm the one who reads your comments. I did make an effort to stop reading the majority of comments in preparation for the Disney week show, but there was no avoiding the tidal wave of opinions that flooded in after the show aired. My costume choice also became a hot topic of discussion in the blogosphere. I may have wanted to bury my head in the sand and ignore it all, but I'm not sure there's a desert big enough!

My one and only dance recital
with my sister Melissa.

Being announced on *GMA*
(Good Morning America)
as a *DWTS* Season 18
contestant!

With my sister Melissa and
three nieces Emma, Molly, and
Kate. They made me a "candy
ball" in honor of my team name
"D.J. Candyball."

We went full throttle
our first week of rehearsals.
There was no easing
into it!

Taking a well-deserved break.

Week 1: Contemporary
(photo courtesy of Adam Taylor, Getty Images)

We got the first 9 of the show!

When I fell asleep at frozen yogurt with my kids after an exhausting week.

Week 2: Rhumba
(photo courtesy of Adam Taylor, Getty Images)

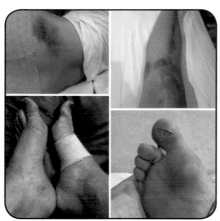

A few of the bruises and cuts I endured during the show. Pretty nasty, I know!

A selfie of us on our phones because we were always on them.

With some of my biggest supports: Left to right: Allison, my
BF Dilini, Stacy, me, my sister Bridgette, and sister Melissa
(photo courtesy of Stacy Williams)

Lori Loughlin and Andrea Barber
came to visit me during rehearsals.

This was right after I took a break
doing the jive to adjust my attitude.
It worked!

On lunch break right
before the big show!
I loved my retro hair.

Scott Weinger (aka Steve) and Andrea Barber (aka Kimmy Gibbler) at the live taping of our most memorable year.

Week 3: Jive
(photo courtesy of Adam Taylor, Getty Images)

Hamming it up for the press after the show. Mark played me like a guitar.

Week 4: Quickstep. Pro partner switch-up with Tony Dovolani. He kept me calm and collected.
(photo courtesy of Adam Taylor, Getty Images)

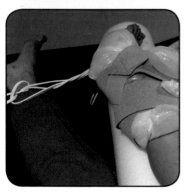

After the show, I celebrated my 38th birthday with family and friends. My youngest son Maks and I loved the cupcakes!

Bruised, sore and trying to prevent a fracture in my foot hours before the live show.

Mark and I reenacting our best Ariel and Sebastian moment.
(photo courtesy of Mark Ballas)

Week 5: Samba
(photo courtesy of Adam Taylor, Getty Images)

Twins! I was so excited to meet Wynonna Judd who was so sweet and encouraging to me!

I had more bruises than I could count!

Caught! Doing pushups right before taking the stage.

I was all nerves, but I
didn't let it show.

Week 6: Cha-Cha-Cha
(photos courtesy of Adam Taylor, Getty Images)

Cast photo! Left to right: Nene Leaks, Mark Ballas, me, James
Maslow, Danika McKeller, Tony Dovolani, Meryl Davis, Peta
Mergatroyd, and Drew Carey

I walked into my dressing room only to find Andrea Barber in my costume! Kimmy and D.J. forever.

Rehearsal selfie where the producers would run the camera and sit at the computer.

This costume was one of my top 3 favorites! Sophisticated and spicy.

Week 7: Argentine Tango—My favorite dance.
(photo courtesy of Adam Taylor, Getty Images)

Backstage selfie with James Maslow. He's such a cutie.

Mark preferred my hair up with my neck exposed for all my ballroom dances so my lines would look elongated.

Week 8: Foxtrot
(photo courtesy of Adam Taylor, Getty Images)

At the wardrobe department getting fit for my costume made from scratch.

Week 8: Dual dance. My feet never touched the ground with my celeb partner Charlie White.
(photo courtesy of Adam Taylor, Getty Images)

Look who's on his phone again! Break time.

I wished the show was called *Gymnastics with the Stars!*

Channeling my inner Broadway girl, Chicago style.

Week 9: Jazz
(photo courtesy of Adam Taylor, Getty Images)

Wig, check.
Confidence . . . still
finding it.

One of my
favorite photos
we took during
the show after
our jazz routine.

Week 9: Waltz. Mark was literally talking me through every single step.
(photo courtesy of Adam Taylor, Getty Images)

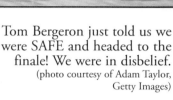

Tom Bergeron just told us we were SAFE and headed to the finale! We were in disbelief.
(photo courtesy of Adam Taylor, Getty Images)

With Angela Thomas after the "American Icons Night" show. She was my angel through the entire journey.

Mark took this photo of me at our final costume fitting just after the "pushing my face incident." I was still so mad and didn't want to look at him, but needed his approval of the dress. He thought my expression was quite hilarious and broke the tension by snapping the pic.
(photo courtesy of Mark Ballas)

This was taken late at night. We were the last ones to leave rehearsals. I was giddy because I was so tired, and Mark just wanted to go home.

Week 10: Quickstep
(photo courtesy of Adam Taylor, Getty Images)

Week 10: Freestyle: Disco
(photo courtesy of Adam Taylor, Getty Images)

Immediately after the finals, I chowed down on pizza with my BF Dilini.

The finale show with some of my prayer warriors: left to right: Andrea B., my sister Melissa, Dilini, Andrea R., Stacy, and Summer.

Rehearsing backstage for our finale fusion dance. I was such a stress ball and Mark was calming me down.
(photo courtesy of Mark Ballas)

I couldn't have done it without my mom's support, prayers and wisdom.

I'm so blessed to be called wife and mom by these four incredibly supportive loves of my life.
(photo courtesy of Andrea Barber)

With my oldest son, Lev.

My all time favorite picture of Mark!! I laugh every time I see it. We were on our way to *Good Morning America* after taking a private jet to New York after the show. None of us had slept in over 24 hours and Mark clearly isn't a morning person.

On *GMA*. This picture sums up our experience together. We had a blast!
(photo courtesy of Adam Taylor, Getty Images)

On our flight home. This photo captures our goofy relationship and one I'll never forget.

- "You're not godly enough."
- "You're not very humble."
- "Your brother, Kirk Cameron, is a better Christian than you."
- "You need Jesus more than ever."
- "You're too worldly."
- "You're not modest enough."
- "You're such a disappointment as a Christian."
- "You're a show-off."
- "We used to look up to you, now you're just like the rest of Hollywood."

That's a sneak peek at the kind of comments that found their way onto my computer screen. I had already resolved to stop worrying about what other people thought about me and my Christian walk and to live my faith on my own, between me and God, but that didn't keep me from being saddened by the culture of criticism and conflict that develops so easily online, particularly from other Christians.

I'm no stranger to criticism. It's a nasty side effect of being a celebrity (and a human being, right?). Over the years, I've had to train myself not to be defensive or reactionary. I've grown a thick skin and figured out how to "Shake It Off" in the words of Taylor Swift.

Instead of defending myself against every critique, I've learned to race toward Psalm 91:1–4.

> The one who lives under the protection of the
>   Most High
> dwells in the shadow of the Almighty.
> I will say to the LORD, "My refuge and my fortress,
> my God, in whom I trust."

He Himself will deliver you from the hunter's net,
from the destructive plague.
He will cover you with His feathers;
you will take refuge under His wings.
His faithfulness will be a protective shield.

God is my refuge! His presence is my safe place to run
when I am under attack. Having the right words at the right
time can't always shield me from criticism. Neither can trying to live like other people want me to. Remember? That's a
snare, not a safety net!

This passage says that God will deliver me from the hunter's net. This passage is describing someone who is especially
good at laying traps. I've certainly encountered a few hunters
online! But God is able to defend me. I don't have to work to
avoid the trap all on my own. He can also protect me against
"the destructive plague," those attacks that come all at once.
That's a pretty good description of the heat I took for some of
the choices I made on the show.

Looking back I can see that part of the reason that Melissa
fought so hard to keep me out of that Ariel costume was that
she was being defensive *for* me. She was trying to shield me
from the potential onslaught of others' criticism she figured
was coming. As my big sister, she wanted to protect me. But
ultimately, she couldn't. God had to be my defender.

Maybe you will never face thousands of critics who are
mad at you for a costume choice. Maybe no one will ever blog
about whether or not your clothes match what you claim to
believe, but the lessons of Psalm 91 still apply to you. You will
face criticism. You will have people in your world who don't
affirm you in the way you want to be affirmed. You will be
misunderstood. Then what?

You can run around trying to counteract every negative comment or opinion, but you will probably just end up exhausted from all the effort required and there's no guarantee that the naysayers will ever see it your way. A better alternative is to seek refuge under the mighty wings of the Lord. To remind yourself often that He is faithful and to hold that faithfulness up as a shield. When God's got your back, you are free to respond to even your harshest critics with grace. You can choose to hold your chin high and reject the temptation to wallow in self-pity or defensiveness.

Even though dealing with the onslaught of public criticism wasn't easy and it's something I continually deal with every day, I wouldn't trade that part of my experience for anything. I look back on this stage of the competition and see that I came out on top on so many different levels. Sure, Mark and I earned some great scores from the judges and I found my inner Disney princess! But more important, I found the confidence in myself to make good decisions, something my track record had already proven each week in the competition and throughout my life. I wouldn't be the woman I am today if it weren't. And I learned that I don't want to be a better, but fake version of myself. I'd never want to lose the elements of compassion, love, and understanding and I always want to be teachable and moldable, but this was a watershed moment for me. I decided that I'd rather be the best Christian with all my flaws and be true to my walk than to live my life so that other people will feel like I'm making the right choices. I found the strength to stand with conviction.

Putting the Shoe on the Other Foot

These are important principles to learn for standing with conviction in the face of criticism. But what about when we are the ones dishing out the critiques? C'mon, girls! I'm not the only one who occasionally watches the choices others are making and thinks, *What were you thinking?* Am I?

There's just something about the Internet that seems to weaken our filter toward what we feel the freedom to say to each other. In reflecting on my experience in dealing with public scrutiny, I didn't want to miss the opportunity to point all of us (me included!) to God's Word for some ground rules for how we treat each other online.

So, before you hit that little button to publish a comment or tweet or take the time to write a blog or share your opinions on someone's Facebook wall, here are three big ideas to keep in mind.

Big Idea #1: Only Build Up

Ephesians 4:29 says, "Let no corrupting talk come out of your mouths, but only such as is good for building up, as fits the occasion, that it may give grace to those who hear" (ESV).

This verse says we should only say what builds others up. Sometimes it seems like we get this totally backward online—only speaking up when we have something negative to say. Before you respond online, train yourself to ask this question, "Does what I am about to say give grace to those who will read it?"

But what if someone really needs to be called out as a Christian? "I'm not judging them," you say, "I'm helping them see that their decisions don't line up with the Bible." See Big Idea #2.

Big Idea #2: Go One-on-One First

Matthew 18:15 gives us our marching orders for how we should treat each other, in person and online. It says, "If your brother sins against you, go and tell him his fault, between you and him alone" (ESV).

As Christians, when we see fault in the lives of other believers, the Bible urges us to approach them one-on-one. We aren't supposed to use public forums to address private grievances. When we do so, we inevitably pull others into the fray. Some people even beg to private message me . . . if only they had private access to me. But the point is, you don't! Private messages are reserved for people who I have personal relationships and friendships with in my life.

In regards to the heat I take online, people often say, "Oh Candace, just delete them and block the haters" or, "Don't let them get to you. Brush it off." But it's not that simple. By the time I decide to get involved (or not to get involved), the comments have been made and read. The bickering back and forth defending me or opposing me has ensued and my Facebook page looks like a war zone. All I see is a bunch of religious people throwing around Bible verses and attacking each other and a bunch of other people saying Christians aren't supposed to judge, citing "Do not judge, so that you won't be judged" (Matt. 7:1), which in my opinion is one of the most grossly misused passages used to counteract online arguments and ultimately leaving a bunch of nonreligious people wondering why in the world they would ever want to be a part of Christianity.

The truth is when we duke it out in a public forum, there is often collateral damage. Committing to always dealing with conflict one-on-one first will limit whose life we have the right to speak in to. *You have to have personal access to someone in order to approach them on this level.* More than likely this means that the Web isn't the right place to express criticism whether they are a public figure or not.

Big Idea #3: Use Careful, Not Careless Words

The Internet may have removed our inhibitions when it comes to what we say (or type), but it doesn't change God's standards.

In Matthew 12:36 Jesus speaks these bold words: "I tell you that on the day of judgment people will have to account for *every careless word they speak"* (emphasis mine).

One day I'm going to have to own up to every comment I fired off in anger and every passive-aggressive tweet I've sent. So will you. With that in mind, we are wise to be careful, not careless, with the way we talk to each other online.

Avoiding the Snare

I wish there was a forever cure for fear of man. If I could bottle the fearlessness and confidence I felt after making the choices that were right for me during Disney week, I would have! I could use a dose of that daily. But the lessons I learned that week have stuck with me.

- Yes, there is wisdom in an abundance of wise counselors, but ultimately my convictions are best formed between me and God.
- I must boldly live my life to please Him and not for the fickle applause of man.
- Fear of man is a trap. If I live my life afraid of what someone might think or say about me, I will trade in

my freedom in Christ for the chains of fear, doubt, worry, resentment, and self-pity.

- Sometimes you have to turn down the voices in order to hear the still, small voice of God.
- God is my defender! I don't have to defend myself.
- I need to be intentional to make sure that my words build up others. I also need to commit to handle conflict in ways that are personal and graceful and make sure my words are carefully chosen, not carelessly dished out.

Off the *DWTS* stage and away from the glaring spotlight, I am resolved that I won't ever stop being the real me to be an illusion of a better but fake Christian version of myself. I don't want to be the poster child for perfection; I want to be a neon sign that points to Jesus. In the days to come, I am likely to disappoint my critics again—that may include some of the readers of this book. But please look to Jesus and only Jesus for perfection. You certainly won't find it in me, and I promise you won't find it in others either. But here's what we can do while we fix our eyes on Jesus . . . we can encourage one another. We can build each other up. We can choose our words wisely to share the truth in love, and we can make a pact to be gracious to others, including those we only know through our computer screens.

After all, "The fear of man is a snare, but the one who trusts in the LORD is protected" (Prov. 29:25).

Chapter 7

In His Image

So God created man in His own image; He created him
in the image of God; He created them male and female.
—GENESIS 1:27

Once I sambaed my way across the stage in mermaid fins, I
felt like I'd already crossed the finish line. Making it through
that week was a huge victory for me, especially since it
was such an upset and shock for Australian pop star Cody
Simpson to be eliminated over me. When the show started, I
set a goal for myself to make it to the halfway point. I knew
going in that my limited dance experience might be a hin-
drance. I didn't want that to lead to my elimination, so I set
a goal to stay in the game until week six. When the cameras
started rolling on the live show that week, and I was still
standing on the *DWTS* stage, I felt like I'd achieved my whole

goal for the show. The finale was still weeks away, but I had already crossed the finish line that I drew for myself.

But every mountain climber will tell you, sometimes it's hard to breathe at the summit. I was proud of my work and thrilled to still be competing, but I was having trouble catching my breath! My nerves were getting worse by the day. I was emotionally exhausted. I started to experience mental blocks where I could not remember my routine. My mind and body had been in a pressure cooker for six long weeks and I was beginning to crack.

The production schedule for each week included two to three full runs of my routine on stage, with cameras on Sundays depending on whether the live band or a track would be playing our song during the live show. Monday mornings were hair and makeup, my final costume fitting, running the routine two times for camera blocking, a full dress rehearsal run, and then, of course, the live show Monday night. Those two days became my most nerve-racking days each week and my anxiety was increasingly getting worse. By week six, I developed a nervous stomach and had to fight waves of nausea before practices and performances. During this week I also started blanking out during the routine. I had never experienced mental blocks before, but suddenly I simply couldn't remember segments of the dance.

Week six was "party anthem week" with Redfoo as guest judge and performer, but it didn't feel like a party to me. Mark and I were assigned the cha-cha-cha, a ballroom dance characterized by small steps, straight legs, and swaying hip movements. We were given "I Love It" by Icona Pop to dance to, but I've got to be honest, I didn't love the way competing at this level was making me feel. I experienced levels of fear and panic that I don't ever want to endure again. I couldn't get through the routine on stage on Sunday without blanking out at times, briefly forgetting where I was in the dance or what I was supposed to be doing. The transition of taking my perfectly rehearsed routine from the rehearsal studio to the *DWTS* stage made me feel disoriented. I had no point of reference that was familiar within my routine and my tired brain was starting to short-circuit.

On Monday morning we got three shots to get through the routine, twice for camera blocking with the band and once for the full dress rehearsal, which is taped. I didn't make it through the entire routine one single time with six tries on stage between the two days. Mark didn't help my situation by becoming frustrated and upset with me. He knew I could do the dance perfectly back at the rehearsal studio and didn't want to just drag me through it with a few missteps on stage. He wanted a perfect run, because even though it was rehearsal he knew everyone was watching and there was a lot of pressure on him as my pro.

At one point I broke down and told Mark that the pressure was simply too much for me. I said, "I think I'm done, dude, I'm just choking." I was ready to throw in the towel. In response, Mark walked off the stage again upset and frustrated with me. I felt those old fears of disappointing others start to rise up in me. I wanted to burst into tears right then and there and I started to. Mark saw it and called out to me, but I just ignored him. Producers came over to reassure me everything would be fine, but I wasn't having it. As soon as possible I made a beeline to my dressing room, where I cried and prayed and desperately e-mailed my prayer team to intercede for me.

Support for Shaky Limbs

It's in those moments when we can't see the forest for the trees—when it looks like the mountain in front of us is insurmountable or our weaknesses cannot be overcome—that we most need the support of others who will love us well and speak God's truth into our lives.

This point is beautifully illustrated in Exodus 17. Moses and the people of God must do battle against the armies of Amalek, a pagan king. Moses gives these marching orders to Joshua, the commander of the Israelite army: "Select some men for us and go fight against Amalek. Tomorrow I will stand on the hilltop with God's staff in my hand" (v. 9).

As the battle raged on, the strangest thing happened. As long as Moses kept his arms in the air, the Israelites kept the upper hand, but when his arms started to drop, Amalek's armies gained ground. No one can hold their arms up hour after hour. Moses' limbs got shaky. His strength was spent. But so much was on the line!

I wasn't in that kind of battle, but I was fighting to be true to myself, to represent Christ well, and to finish strong. But my limbs were shaking. My strength was zapped. My courage was waning.

What did Moses do? He literally leaned on the strength of others.

"When Moses' hands grew heavy, they took a stone and put it under him, and he sat down on it. Then Aaron and Hur supported his hands, one on one side and one on the other so that his hands remained steady until the sun went down. So Joshua defeated Amalek and his army with the sword" (vv. 12–13).

I leaned hard into the arms of several people as my mental battle intensified. Val was an important "pillar" for me, of course. He had competed on a similar reality TV competition show called *Battle of the Blades* as a pro hockey player turned pair's figure skating competitor with Olympic gold medalist Ekaterina Gordeeva, so he knew a lot about the experience. He absorbed as much of the pressure as possible and reminded me that we were running this race as a family. Stacy, my personal prayer partner for the past several years, faithfully encouraged me, prayed for me, and cheered me on. My best friend, Dilini, also comforted me and was a listening ear at every stage of the journey. And my prayer team was still praying like crazy! Without these people "holding up my arms" I simply wouldn't have been able to go on past week five. Even when I couldn't see it, they helped me to remember that the finish line wasn't nearly as important as how I ran the race. I wanted to run well!

Some of you are in a battle as you read these words. Maybe you've lost the high ground. Maybe it's a diagnosis that's knocked you flat, or a relationship gone south, or a sin you can't seem to get victory over. If that's you, you know what it's like to feel your strength get zapped and your limbs get shaky. But my guess is, that fat lady's not singing yet! There's most likely still a battle to be fought. No, you probably cannot do it on your own, but you don't have to. Who can shore you up? Who can point you toward God's truth when you cannot seem to grasp it for yourself? Don't be afraid to reach your arms toward the people in your world who can love and encourage you and can help stabilize your heart during times of war.

Finding My Inner Pussycat Doll?

I was just trying to tread enough water to stay afloat, but soon I had a new challenge to face. As Mark and I practiced the cha-cha-cha, he kept saying things to me like:

"You got to own your sexy girl."
"You've gotta sell it and make every guy in the room, like 'Aaaoooo-gguh!'"
"Just strut your stuff."
"Pretend you're a Pussycat Doll."

But here's the problem. I am most definitely *not* a Pussycat Doll! I am a mother of three, more accustomed to carpools than the club scene. It wasn't that Mark had choreographed a sexy or provocative dance, but to take on the roll of this dance, it required sexy hip movement and a level of confidence that was really hard for me. At the end of the dance, I was supposed to snap my finger and strut toward the audience. It was so hard for me to "own it" like Mark wanted me to.

As we rehearsed, we'd get to the strut and Mark would stop me every time.

"Lame. You look like my grandma," he'd say.
"Not attractive."
"Not sexy."

I could laugh it off, but there was no denying this was a difficult thing for me. I started to get very discouraged because I didn't want to look like a grandma, but I simply didn't feel sexy.

Before I knew it, insecurities I had previously been unaware of started to bubble up to the surface.

As I've said before, of course I do feel like it's important to reserve sex and certain parts of myself for my husband. Somewhere along the line I think I also decided to hide away parts of my femininity and confidence as a woman. I recognized that a part of me felt like I was never allowed to embrace my sexuality and my femininity in its fullest form because when you're a Christian it's something you reserve for one man.

> Mark gave me the nickname "Edna Flemington" because I reminded him of an old lady and was constantly clearing my throat. What can I say, I had lots of phlegm!

Before any feathers get ruffled out there, let me reiterate that Mark and I weren't trying to create a sexy dance. And while I was trying to come to terms with how to express my own sexuality, it's worth noting that not all sexuality is God-honoring and worthy of embracing. I wanted to stick within the biblical guidelines for sex, without ignoring that I am created as a sexual creature. Sex is God's idea, after all. So are manhood and womanhood. As I tried and failed to walk across that stage as a confident woman, I had to wrestle with the fact that I didn't feel like I had the freedom to own who I was.

> The cha-cha-cha was my most memorable dance, not because I loved it so much, but because I never wanted to feel the way I felt during this round of competition again. Mentally, it was the toughest week of my *DWTS* journey.

What Is Womanhood *Really* About?

Take a man (or woman!) on the street, poll them about womanhood, and you're likely to discover that I'm not the only one with hesitations about what womanhood should look like. Depending on who you ask, you might hear answers like:

- Women are supposed to be tender and nurturing.
- Women are supposed to be strong and sexy.
- Women should be responders.
- Women should be initiators.
- Women should be gentle and quiet.
- Women should be bold and powerful.

No wonder I was second-guessing myself. If we try to live up to the world's standards for womanhood, we'll all get whiplash.

But what matters most is not how the culture defines womanhood, or even how I define womanhood. What matters most is God's plan for my design—*He* is the designer.

In Genesis 1:27 we see God's master plan for gender:

So God created man in His own image; He created him in the image of God; He created them male and female.

Men and women were created *in the image of God*. From the beginning we see men and women created uniquely. Our parts are not interchangeable, neither are our God-given roles. Men and women are given equal value, both bearing the image of God, and both formed by the hand of a loving Creator. But the genders were designed to communicate different parts of the image of God. Who I am as a woman is unique and separate from who my husband is as a man. When

I hide my womanhood or apologize for it, I'm covering up the image of God I was designed to portray.

As I write this, I'm almost forty years old, and I still struggle with feeling like a little girl sometimes. Can anyone else relate?

I had to face questions like:

Am I glad that I'm a woman?

Is it good that I'm a woman?

How can I express my God-given femininity and still honor God's plan for my sexuality?

I realized that I don't like it when Christian women feel the need to hide themselves completely—when we are embarrassed because we have a body, complete with hips and curves. I'm not talking about dressing or acting provocatively here. I hope I've established that I highly value the qualities of modesty and discretion, but as I struggled to just *walk* confidently I realized that I didn't have to hide my femininity. I didn't have to hide my confidence as a woman because I am an image-bearer of God.

It wasn't sexiness that I was searching for; it was confidence. As a Christian woman I've been told to hold my sexuality and femininity back. To keep it hidden. But somehow it ended up being my confidence that got stuffed down. Because of this dance and the way that Mark was talking me through it, I had to find my confidence as a woman or fall flat on my face in front of millions. I had to take a hard look at what the Bible really teaches about my femininity and come to terms with what it means to bear God's image.

Biblically Bold

I learned that it's a misunderstanding of femininity that we think biblical femininity is only reserved, bashful, or plain. As I dug deep looking for confidence, I wondered, *What is the context for a godly woman to be bold?*

I didn't have to look any further than the Bible for my answer. Here's a quick look at some of my favorite bold women in God's Word.

Deborah the Prophetess

Deborah's story is found in Judges 4–5. The Bible tells us that Deborah was married and that she served as a judge for the people of Israel. An enemy named Sisera made threats against God's people, but God had promised deliverance. There was only one problem; Israel's general, Barak, was too afraid to lead the charge. Deborah wanted to see her people win the victory that God had promised, so she boldly reminded Barak what was at stake:

> Move on, for this is the day the LORD has handed Sisera over to you. Hasn't the LORD gone before you? (Judg. 4:14)

Deborah used bold confidence to point Barak back to God's promises. Apparently he needed the reminder, because he changed from a weak leader to a commanding general, wiping out the entire enemy army. That's the power of a confident woman!

Ruth the Desperate Widow

Ruth's story is told in the Old Testament book of Ruth. After her husband and father-in-law died, Ruth accompanied her mother-in-law, Naomi, to Judah. There, Ruth and Naomi struggled to make ends meet as two widows.

Through hard work and a bold move, Ruth secured a "kinsman redeemer" in a man named Boaz. Boaz married Ruth, provided for her and Naomi, and fathered Ruth's son, Obed. Obed went on to become the grandfather of King David, securing Ruth's place in the lineage of Jesus.

But Ruth did not just sit back and wait for all of this to happen to her. She boldly approached Boaz and asked for his help.

Anna the Prayer Warrior

Anna's story doesn't get much real estate in the Bible, just two short verses in Luke 2:36–38, but that doesn't mean that Anna wasn't bold.

The Bible tells us that Anna was "advanced in years" (ESV). Which is just a nice way of saying Anna was old, somewhere in her eighties or nineties. For decades Anna lived in the temple and watched and prayed for the Savior she knew was coming to redeem her people from their sin.

Because she had so much practice praying bold prayers, she knew the Savior when she saw Him. He arrived at the temple when He was just a few weeks old and wrapped in His mama's arms.

When she saw Jesus, she boldly proclaimed His divinity: "At that very moment, she came up and began to thank God and to speak about Him to all who were looking forward to the redemption of Jerusalem" (Luke 2:38).

Anna didn't timidly talk about Jesus. She didn't whisper that He had arrived. She fearlessly shouted it from the rooftops.

Beautiful Fierceness

There's no cookie-cutter version of femininity to be found in the lives of these women. There are single girls, married women, and widows represented in these stories. Some had to boldly fight for what they needed to survive; others used their lives to boldly point others to God. Some seemed to be naturally confident, and others had to be encouraged to speak up. All are a part of God's story because they are women who bore His image well.

What these women had was a beautiful fierceness.

Kimberly Wagner writes about that fierce woman this way: "She is a warrior at heart—not violent or aggressive—but tempered by humility. She's a soft warrior; fleshing out the beauty of fierceness in her daily life. Loving God and others with sacrificial devotion. . . . I love to see a fierce woman in action."[9]

Kimberly goes on to outline the characteristics of a beautifully fierce woman:

- Her identity and value are rooted in her relationship with Christ rather than a relationship with a man.
- She's filled with gratitude for God's good gifts. Her heart is ruled by the peace of contentment.
- She courageously faces her fears rather than running or hiding in shame.
- She's passionate about things that matter rather than living for the trivial.
- She loves God and others. She's more focused on giving love than getting love.
- She's willing to battle for a worthy cause rather than shrinking in defeat.

- She grabs the hem of God's will and doesn't let go.
- She protects and defends the helpless rather than using her strength to bully others. She is known as a sincere encourager.
- She's honest but kind.
- Others feel comfortable in seeking her counsel.
- She embraces God's Word as her ultimate authority rather than being swayed by the voices of the culture.
- She faithfully confronts by speaking truth in love rather than enabling sin by keeping silent.
- She walks in confidence and humility that flow from her recognition of Christ's work of grace in her life.
- She has the power to influence and inspire because she lives under the Spirit's control.
- Her life is lived all out for God's glory rather than the smallness of self.[10]

What a list! Now that's a brand of femininity I can embrace! Instead of hiding who I am as a woman, I want to bear God's image with beautiful fierceness. Don't you?

As I wrestled with what God's Word says about my femininity, sexuality, and design, I discovered a newfound freedom to embrace being a beautiful, confident woman without being fearful or ashamed of it. And you know what? Confidence is attractive. There's just something about a confident woman that makes others want to perk up and take notice.

Once again, I had to face the fact that I care about what other people think about me to my detriment. Fear of being perceived as provocative kept the beautiful fierceness He intends for me to display under wraps.

The message my womanhood is designed to send is not, "I'm hot. I'm sexy and I'm in control," but rather, "I'm confident in who God made me to be. He knew what He was doing! He is in control!" And that confidence doesn't just make people take notice of me; it makes people take notice of my God and puts Him on display!

Shame versus Convictions

I wanted to dance in a way that declared, "I am a woman. I am proud of who God made me to be." To get there I had to address the difference between conviction and shame. My convictions were strong beliefs based on what I read in God's Word. During this part of the journey I realized that some of the things I thought were convictions were really rooted in shame. Being a strong woman or a bold woman felt like something I needed to hide.

The lives of the women outlined on the previous page prove that being bold doesn't have to mean that you're sassy or provocative, and it doesn't discriminate against physical beauty. Some of them had a quiet confidence, others were more outspoken. All were created with femininity and sexuality, but they didn't use those as weapons to get what they wanted. Instead they pointed others to God in ways that only a woman could. They are beautiful examples of what it means to bear the image of God. They teach us that being a confident woman looks different for each of us. In this moment, I simply needed enough confidence to snap my fingers and cha-cha-cha across the stage. That probably looks different in your life, but we have the freedom to be confident women without shame.

Ultimately, when the lights went on and the cameras started to roll for the week six live show, I did it! I got through my entire routine without any noticeable glitches and, most of all, I had fun! I could only attribute it to all the prayers that had been sent up on my behalf. I even pointed up to the sky and thanked the Lord during the post interview. I don't know that Mark ever hugged me with relief harder than he did that night. He was so glad I made it through the whole dance and reminded me of how proud he was that I overcame my fear, pushed through, and had a good time while I was doing it.

The judges did notice the tension I was experiencing between wanting to own my femininity and feeling uncomfortable about showcasing my sexuality.

Bruno declared, "Candace, you are sexy. You just don't know it."

He pointed out that he could almost see me wrestling with exhibiting confidence and then stopping myself, looking like a switch that was being flipped on and off. He encouraged me to keep the current running through all the time because it was there! The other judges agreed and offered encouragement if I advanced to the next round, which I did, but not without being in jeopardy in the bottom two once again.

Obviously, this is an area where I don't have everything figured out, but I'm making progress. I've always known who I am and Whose I am, and *DWTS* helped me to "own it" and to be confident in who God made me to be. With that hard lesson learned, I can look back on week six and see that our song choice was perfect . . . "I Love It!"

Chapter 8

Letting Go of Perfect

Therefore, I will most gladly boast all the
more about my weaknesses, so that Christ's
power may reside in me.
—2 CORINTHIANS 12:9

Four words have the power to simultaneously strike terror into my heart and fill me with pure excitement—Colossus at Magic Mountain. Back in the day it was the tallest and fastest wooden roller coaster in the world and the first with two drops greater than 100 feet. I rode Colossus for the first time as a terrified twelve-year-old. I'd technically been tall enough to ride the two previous times I'd been to the theme park but I could never muster up enough courage to get on. My sisters and my friends tried to talk me into it, but my fear was just too great and I'd always cop out right before it was our turn to be seated. But finally, after my group of friends and family had ridden Colossus once and were going back for a second run, I decided to go for it. I was determined. There was no going back!

I was absolutely scared to death. I wanted to panic as the lap bar locked into place. The train started to move and clicked its way up every notch toward the first and biggest drop. My friends told me to put my hands in the air, but instead I gripped the bar so tightly my knuckles turned white. I concentrated on keeping myself from throwing up and crying all at the same time. My mom told me to scream. She said, "Let the air out. It will help you breathe and have fun." So I did. I screamed as loud and as hard as I could as the coaster rolled up and down for a wild two minutes and thirty seconds.

When the ride finished, I breathed a sigh of relief. And then let out a big, "Whoo Hoo!" My smile was plastered across my face and I felt so empowered! I loved it! It was exhilarating and exciting that I pushed through my fears. At that moment, I felt unstoppable. The Colossus taught me that I could accomplish anything, even if it scared me.

That ride was such a triumph that I wanted to ride roller coasters everywhere. As I traveled for work making appearances in cities all over the country during my *Full House* years, my manager organized some play time for me at each city's greatest theme park. My goal was to ride all the biggest and baddest roller coasters in the country. And just like a roller coaster ride, there were ups and downs trying so many of them. Some were great and some made me sick, but the risk never stopped me from trying.

As the weeks whizzed by on *DWTS*, I felt like I'd strapped in for a ride much more terrifying and exhilarating than my run on the Colossus. When week seven arrived and

I was still a member of the *DWTS* cast, a part of me felt like I'd just taken a 100-foot drop. My stomach was in my throat and I was freaking out a bit that I was still on the ride. The range of emotions I experienced each week sure felt like a roller-coaster ride. One minute I thought, *Oh, I can't believe I made it! This is so exciting!* The next minute I'd think, *I want off the show! This is so hard and I'm scared to death to go out there and perform. What if blanking out becomes a new thing for me each week? I can't do this!* One moment I'd be picturing myself in the finals, and the next moment I'd imagine forgetting my entire routine while millions of people watched. By making it to this point, I had surpassed my goal and that was fantastic. But my nerves were shot, my body was spent, and my emotions were totally haywire.

My struggles were obvious. Mark said, "I've never dealt with anyone with nerves like yours in all my past contestants." Apparently when it came to the grueling mental game that comes with being on the show, I was in a league of my own!

After I started blanking out on set, the producers also took notice. Realizing that I was losing the battle to control my anxiety, they suggested that I go see a sport psychologist.

> Our dance for week seven was the Argentine tango. This partner dance is characterized by partners moving counterclockwise around the dance floor in a close hold. It was developed in African-Argentine dance venues by "compadritos." Picture a young South American man with a slouch hat, loosely tied neckerchief, high-heeled boots, and a knife tucked casually in his belt.[11]

People who watched the show have since asked me if that was a suggestion made out of genuine concern or an attempt to create a story line. I can say with absolute certainty that the producers weren't trying to boost ratings or paint me as a contestant who had gone off her rocker. They were genuinely concerned that I was cracking under the pressure. Two particular producers, both women, were very nice and nurturing toward me throughout the entire journey. They showed genuine concern for my well-being. They could see it in my eyes that I wasn't coping well, and they intervened for my benefit.

In hindsight I can also see that they knew how many people were voting for me each week. I didn't have access to those numbers. Along the way a couple of people implied that my voting base was strong enough to get me to the finish line, saying things like, "Trust me, you're not going anywhere." (Wink. Wink.) What can I say? I have the best fans in the whole world! But I couldn't process any of that in the moment. I was simply too exhausted. The producers knew that my fans would keep me in it for the long haul. I believe setting up an appointment with a sport psychologist was their attempt to help me mentally stay in the game.

Since none of our other efforts to calm my nerves and stop the blackouts seemed to be working, Mark and I agreed to go to the therapist, but we were skeptical. We secretly wondered if we'd even be seeing a real sport psychologist, or just some celebrity version.

The Doctor Will See You Now

Despite our reservations, Mark and I headed off to therapy. I had never seen a psychologist before. My plan was to play it smart. I was going to give the producers something they could use for my video package, but I had no intentions of actually revealing anything deeply personal about myself while the world watched. My guard was way up.

Mark and I plopped onto the couch in a very small therapy office. We were sitting side by side, but we weren't exactly cozy. There was probably a foot or more of space between us. As close as Mark and I had grown in friendship over the past two months, it was weird to be sitting in therapy with someone that was still pretty new to my life. We had to chuckle at the reality of what reality television can bring you to do. The therapist sitting across from us was Dr. Jenn Mann, formerly known as Dr. Jenn Berman, an accomplished psychotherapist and sport psychology consultant who also has her own TV show on VH1. *Great*, I thought disappointedly, *we are seeing a celebrity doctor*, and any expectation or hope of the session actually helping went out the door.

Three would have been a crowd in that small space, but we still had all of the cameras and producers to cram in. There was a camera on the therapist, one on Mark, one on me, and one tasked with getting a wide shot of Mark and me together. An operator manned each of the four cameras and two producers joined us. In case you lost count, that meant that nine people were in the room where I was supposed to pour my heart out. This wasn't exactly private practice!

All of that solidified my plan to protect myself. I didn't want to expose anything while the whole world watched. (At least it *felt* like the whole world was watching!) It wasn't that I was hiding any big secrets, but I was definitely leery of oversharing. I wanted to be honest, but I didn't want to fillet myself out there for everyone to pick apart.

The session started with typical therapist questions like you hear in movies. Picture me on a couch responding to, "How does that make you feel?"

I answered honestly, but she kept digging for mommy and daddy issues. I put an end to that pretty quickly, telling her, "You're not going to find anything there!" I knew that if she went burrowing through the closets of my childhood, she wouldn't find any skeletons. No childhood is perfect, but I grew up in a loving and supportive home. It didn't matter how deep she dug, I knew she wouldn't discover anything different.

She seemed to pivot and started asking about my experience as a child actor. At first, I gave her very surface answers. But she kept prodding and eventually she found a soft spot. My tough exterior started to crack when Dr. Jenn honed in on my deep fear of disappointing others. I'm sure you've picked up on the fact that I care about what others think of me—sometimes too much. In that cramped therapy office, with cameras zoomed in on my face watching my every move, I started to understand why. Dr. Jenn said, "Even though you've been acting your whole life, the kids who tend to do really well as actors growing up, tend to be more 'type A' kids who are perfectionists. Do you feel you have those types of perfectionist traits?" And I answered, "Not when it comes to my personal life, like being a friend, mom, or wife. But when it comes to work and my performance, yes I think I am a perfectionist." The roots of my need to please go back to my job as a child actor. Impressing others was the gig. I learned my lines and I performed my little heart out, always with the goal of hearing the director say, "Well done, Candace. That was great. You were amazing!"

I wanted the producers to give me a pat on the back. I wanted my mom and dad to say "great job." Not because of any pressures that any one person put on me, but just because of the nature of the work, my childhood became very performance based. My singular focus was to do a good job.

Let me stop right here and say that this is not the lament of another child actor, bemoaning life in the spotlight. Just because there was pressure associated with being a child actor, doesn't mean I didn't enjoy it. I loved every minute of it! Some child actors are bitter about having to perform at that level so young. I'm not. I wouldn't change my childhood for something more typical, but there's no denying it molded who I am. Even as a little girl, I learned to like a job well done. I want to please whomever I'm working for or have a relationship with. When that doesn't happen or I feel like I've disappointed someone in my world, I tend to take it harder than most.

Repeating Life Lessons

None of this was groundbreaking. Learning to temper my fear of man was an overarching theme throughout my *DWTS* journey, but these lessons were so tough I needed to learn them over and over again. Sure, it would be great to figure it out once and be done with it, but learning rarely happens that way.

This certainly wasn't the first time that I needed some extra "tutoring" to grasp a difficult lesson. Let's flash back to middle school for a minute. Math has always been hard for me. I remember taking Algebra in eighth grade and having to relearn some basic math skills like simple multiplication and division. My schooling was unusual while I worked on *Full*

House, combining some classes in public school with a private tutor on set, so I somehow missed some math basics in sixth and seventh grade that prevented me from understanding and moving forward in algebra. Not to mention, numbers just hurt my brain! I'm much more naturally suited for creative thinking. It felt like a massive task to pass Algebra I. I struggled through every problem and formula. I dreaded it, but I put in the hours relearning basic math skills so that I could then try to wrap my brain around new concepts. It was tedious, but with the help of my set teacher, I was able to pass the class and move on to Algebra II.

The stakes were higher now. I wasn't learning algebra, I was learning how to compete on the biggest platform I'd ever been on, but the process was the same. Laying down my need to please, avoiding the trap set by fear of man, and letting myself off the hook of perfection didn't come naturally. But I had to learn those basic life skills in order to move on. Dr. Jenn was my tutor and I was suddenly ready to learn.

We started discussing my need to please and the dam of tears I was determined to hold back broke. Mentally I was kicking myself because the cameras were rolling, but I couldn't help but share because I was suddenly thinking about old issues in brand-new ways.

"This is about you letting go of your insecurities. This is about you letting go of what other people think. This is about you learning to accept your imperfections. If you don't do that, this week will be your last dance." As Dr. Jenn said those words, the floodgates of tears couldn't be stopped.

Let me reiterate that I love my mom and dad. They are wonderful parents who gave me a blessed childhood, but as we started talking more about the issues of confidence and expectations, I realized that in our house mediocrity was okay, sometimes even encouraged as long as it kept things steady. Boldness and confidence wasn't something that was modeled frequently; instead keeping life within the boundaries of consistency was. During my early days as an actress, my dad would say things like, "Why would you want to choose such a difficult career path? There are hundreds of girls competing for the same thing as you, many of whom are even more talented. You're always going to be disappointed when you don't get the part. Why do that to yourself?"

There's no doubt that the pressure that comes along with the entertainment business is real and daunting. My dad had a hard time understanding why I would subject myself to that kind of pressure. He'd often encourage me to quit the entertainment industry and find a stable job because the competition was so stiff.

Looking back I can see that he was trying to manage expectations. Nobody wants their little girl to be disappointed, and I'm sure that he thought that lowering the bar would protect me from shooting for the moon; but it didn't. I still wanted to act and I still wanted someone to believe I could achieve higher goals for myself. But instead, what I learned was to question and doubt myself every step of the way. I learned that the fear of failure outweighed the possibility of trying to succeed.

In contrast, my husband, Val, is one of the most confident people I've ever met, which was one of my initial attractions to him. He's a world-class professional athlete with two Olympic medals to his name whose talent and confidence have taken him far in life. He lives by the motto "excuses are for losers." This is a man that doesn't take the first no for an answer and continues to push and pursue life with an "all-in" attitude. Failure isn't a consideration when it comes to trying. He would never defeat himself mentally before giving it his all and would agree with Michael Jordan when he said, "I can accept failure, everyone fails at something. But I can't accept not trying." So, compare a childhood focused on lowering expectations and a lack of displayed confidence and encouragement to rise above and a marriage to someone with extremely high expectations and a no-lose attitude, and the contrast is pretty dramatic.

So when it came to my relationship with Mark, with a tissue in hand, I told him from my heart, "I want to be the best for you. I know this journey is supposed to be for me, but you're my partner. I want the two of us to get to the end! I never want to be the reason of disappointment because I'm an encourager by nature and I'm a happy person, so when I feel like I'm holding someone back (that'd be Mark as a dance pro in this case) or pulling someone down (to a lower level of performance standards) that makes me feel terrible." I felt like I'd let him down somewhere along the line.

Some of the teary stuff the producers caught on camera actually came from me talking about my dad and my husband. Since those are two of my favorite people in the entire world and I want to honor them, I asked the producers not to show the footage where I discussed those relationships. In the end they edited two and a half hours of footage down to a very short clip that focused on my fear of disappointing Mark. The tears were real. The issues were real. And the impact was very real.

By the end of the session, Mark's arm was around me. We were sitting side by side and he was comforting me in a very big brother kind of way. We had had a breakthrough!

A Game Changer

As we were leaving Dr. Jenn's office, Mark said, "I thought that was going to be a joke, but it was pretty great."

I totally agreed. I didn't expect to learn anything new about myself. I certainly didn't expect a mental break-through, but I was pleasantly surprised to walk out of that office with a new perspective and new tools for the journey going forward. Dr. Jenn was pretty fantastic.

Ultimately, that session had a dramatic impact on my relationship with Mark and my ability to perform on the *DWTS* stage. Mark's attitude was different toward me after that week. The way he would pressure me on Sundays and Mondays changed from that point forward. I felt empowered by gaining new insight into what made me tick, and I saw Mark make a conscious effort to teach me and interact with me differently.

I was so appreciative of Mark at that point for listening and responding. Anyone can hear something and just leave it. Mark had a front-row seat to the fact that I have some pretty clear issues about disappointing others. He could have filed that away in his "who cares" file and continued to push me toward perfection. But he didn't. He saw what the hurdles were and made a decision to course-correct.

In this way Mark modeled for me a skill that I want to bring into my own relationships off the dance floor. People have needs. They have worries and fears. They have issues that they need to work through. It's easy for me to gloss over that and simply hope they will get over the hump. But I watched Mark take an active role in that session and then change how he taught me beyond that moment. He made the choice to be the best partner that he could be for me in the journey to succeed. What a perfect example for the model of marriage.

Mark's Take

After the show, I wanted to hear what the experience had been like for Mark, straight from the horse's mouth. I traded in my dancin' shoes for a reporter's hat and asked Mark what it was like to share a spot on a counselor's couch with me.

Me: What was that counseling session like for you?

Mark: I thought when we were going in that it was going to be this quick setup thing and about dancing. I was going in there thinking, *This is dumb, this isn't going to work, and how's it going to help me with whatever dance we had that week?* And then we were in there for ten minutes and I was like, *This is kind of insightful,* and then another fifteen to twenty minutes and I thought, *This is actually quite insightful and might be good to bring out some other stuff,* and then . . . it got really deep. The audience didn't see everything in the package that kind of came out, but we went on an emotional roller coaster!

Me: Was it hard for you to change how you coached me?

Mark: No, not after I understood fully where you were at mentally with the challenge. In the first few weeks yes, it was difficult, because I couldn't understand why the first week was so perfect and then the rest of the weeks you were starting to get nervous. After we flushed out all that stuff in the therapy session, I understood. It's important to remember that this show is about your journey, not my journey. And once I understood that this was a huge element of your journey and not some random thing you were doing, I had to be content with that.

Here are the simple tools Dr. Jenn gave me for overcoming performance anxiety:

1. Visualize the routine.

2. Take several long, deep breaths. (This calms your heart rate.)

3. Speak confident phrases to yourself. Instead of saying, "I hope I do well," tell yourself, "I can do this!"

4. Remind yourself that you know what you're doing. You have access to your brain, and all the information you need is stored in there.

Something to Brag About

I've had many fans tell me that those moments in the therapist's office were a turning point for them as well. Instead of being turned off by an area of exposed weakness, they wanted to root for me more, because I was transparent. They didn't say, "You're a mess! You don't belong on that stage." Instead they said, "I really want you to do well because you've got some junk and you owned it, and that's a hard thing to do!"

I was surprised how many people resonated with the fact I had to trade in some of the high expectations I put on myself in an attempt to be perfect for realistic expectations. I think as women we often assume that people will be most impressed by us if we can appear like we've got it all together. Instead, people are drawn to humility, transparency, vulnerability, and even weakness.

It may sound mysterious, and even a little crazy, but God's Word tells us that if we are going to brag about anything, it should be our weaknesses, not our strengths.

In 2 Corinthians 11–12, Paul is writing to the church in Corinth when he finds a strange thing to brag about. "If boasting is necessary, I will boast about my weaknesses" (11:30).

Boast about weakness? Who does that? Paul does. If we keep reading, we find out why.

Paul explains that he has an area of fragility that he can't seem to overcome. He calls it a "thorn in the flesh." Maybe it was a physical weakness. Maybe it was an area of insecurity. Maybe it was a gravitation toward sin. Either way, Paul had a hurdle that he could not overcome on his own. He asked the Lord to take it away. Instead, he learned a valuable lesson about falling short:

> Concerning this, I pleaded with the Lord three times to take it away from me. But He said to me, "My grace is sufficient for you, for power is perfected in weakness." (2 Cor. 12:8–9)

Weaknesses are a good thing because they work like neon signs, pointing out our need for Jesus. Those things that drive us to our knees are a gift because we find the great Need-Meeter there.

If I could wave a magic wand and be free of my imperfections, believe me I would. If I could shed fear of disappointing man completely, I'd do it in a heartbeat. But I cannot. Those patterns are deeply ingrained and a part of who I am. Only God can change my heart, and this journey helped me see how desperately I need Him to do so.

This chapter of the story could have had a completely different ending. I could have kept my heart under lock and key, refusing to acknowledge my weaknesses or discuss my insecurities. I could have applied another layer of glue to my mask of perfection in the hopes that the world would love me more if I could just convince them I was all right. I could have continued to try to be brave in front of Mark, never letting him see my vulnerabilities and fears. I could try to polish myself up to a high shine before approaching Jesus instead of letting Him know just how desperately I need Him.

Imagine how this leg of the journey would have turned out if that was the path I had chosen. Mark and I would have continued to struggle with my intense fear of disappointing others. He would have unknowingly continued to press in harder, making it worse. I would have continued to wrestle with intense anxiety and fear without understanding the root cause. Fans might have watched me and thought I had it all together, but it would have been an act. Instead they got to see the real me. I'm so grateful for the love and support they showed as a result.

Being open about my weakness marked a turning point in the journey for me. If I had refused to get real, I doubt the story would have ended as happily.

Perhaps this is why Paul decided to brag about his flaws:

But He said to me, "My grace is sufficient for you, for power is perfected in weakness." Therefore, I will most gladly boast all the more about my weaknesses, so that Christ's power may reside in me. (2 Cor. 12:9)

When we brag about our frailty, we shine the spotlight on the strength of our God. That's why embracing and sharing our weaknesses is a theme in His Word. Romans 8:26 says that the Spirit helps us in our weakness. First Corinthians 15:43 promises that what is sown in weakness will be raised in power. Don't you remember singing about this in Sunday school? We are weak, but He is strong! The cracks in our perfection provide a place for God's power to rush in and for His name to be glorified!

The Comeback Kid

Ultimately, the week wasn't about falling short. It became a week of triumph. I faced my fears and I hung in there. I wanted to quit, but I didn't and I felt so rewarded. Latin Week proved to be a breakthrough week and our Argentine tango dance to the song "1977" by Ana Tijoux ended up being my favorite dance of the entire season. I wasn't nervous. I didn't blank out. Instead of fixating on my fears and allowing anxiety to control emotions, mind, and body, I felt total freedom to enjoy the ride.

> Play back the tape! Mark yelled "elbow" to me right in the middle of our Argentine tango to remind me to get my elbows out in front of me.

This week also marked the first week I'd be performing two dances! The remaining contestants were split into two groups, chosen by the two teams' captains, Meryl Davis and Charlie White, who were leading in scores. Our Team Loca consisted of Meryl Davis and Maks Chmerkovskiy, Danica McKellar and Val Chmerkovskiy, Amy Purdy and Derek Hough, and Mark and me. We performed to "Livin' La Vida Loca" by Ricky Martin who was guest judging that week, and got a near-perfect score with three 10s and one 9.

When it came to the Argentine tango with Mark, I recalled those simple tools from Dr. Jenn and instead of lowering the bar for myself by saying things like, "I hope I do well," or, "I want to do well," I told myself, "I can do this and I will do this!" I wasn't trying to leap over some impossibly high standard created by the expectations of others. I was free to do my best and untethered from an unrealistic fear of failure.

In the end I got great scores, an 8 and three 9s. That felt good! But the real victory came from the way God was able to work in my heart when I got real about areas of struggle. As the week wrapped, I felt like twelve-year-old Candace on Colossus. I had faced my fears. I'd been high and low in front of a watching world, and God was with me every step of the way.

How about you? Do you have weaknesses you are terrified to expose? Do you build walls in an attempt to keep people from seeing the "real you"? If so, let me encourage you to take Paul's advice. Instead of hiding your flaws, brag about them!

> To envision my character for the heart of the Argentine tango, I referred to my favorite fiction book, *Redeeming Love* by Francine Rivers. In my mind, I was playing Angel the prostitute and Mark was playing the part of Michael Hosea. The book *Redeeming Love* is a retelling of the powerful story of Gomer and Hosea in the Bible.

When we're honest about ourselves and our shortcomings, we shine the light on our God who meets all our needs. Isn't it freeing to know that our imperfections can point others to Jesus? Let go of perfect and grab on to a strong God who loves you just the way you are! What are you waiting for?!

But He said to me, "My grace is sufficient for you, for power is perfected in weakness." Therefore, I will most gladly boast all the more about my weaknesses, so that Christ's power may reside in me. So I take pleasure in weaknesses, insults, catastrophes, persecutions, and in pressures, because of Christ. For when I am weak, then I am strong. (2 Cor. 12:9–10)

Chapter 9

The Livin' Is Easy

He lets me lie down in green pastures;
He leads me beside quiet waters.
—PSALM 23:2

The book of Psalms reads like a series of journal entries to God. Written mostly by the great King David, it's full of gut-wrenching honesty about the ups and downs of life. My tear-filled therapy session was tame compared to the raw emotion that David often wrote with. Here's a taste:

> LORD, how long will You forget me?
> Forever?
> How long will You hide Your face from me?
> How long will I store up anxious concerns within
>   me,
> agony in my mind every day?
> How long will my enemy dominate me? (Ps. 13:1–2)

I am weary from my crying;
my throat is parched.
My eyes fail, looking for my God. (Ps. 69:3)

David knew how to emote! He's a therapist's dream, an open book who wore his heart on his sleeve.

But when you look at the entire book of Psalms, you see that David wasn't always lamenting. He didn't only cry out to God when he was weary and worn out. He didn't only write songs when his heart was full of sorrow and his enemies were at the gate. In fact, much of the Psalms are joyful expressions of gratitude and contentment.

My heart is confident, God;
I will sing; I will sing praises
with the whole of my being.
Wake up, harp and lyre!
I will wake up the dawn.
I will praise You, Lord, among the peoples;
I will sing praises to You among the nations.
For Your faithful love is higher than the heavens,
and Your faithfulness reaches to the clouds.
    (Ps. 108:1–4)

Here David's heart is ready to burst with joy and gratitude. He can't wait for the sun to come up so he can face the day, a stark contrast from when his eyes and throat hurt from crying so much.

I love that David didn't sanitize his prayers and that we have access to them through God's Word, because they represent what life and faith are really like for all of us. There are definitely times when life is hard and we feel like we are climbing that 100-foot peak on the roller coaster or plummeting downward in an out-of-control free fall. But life isn't always like that. Sometimes everything is coming up roses.

Things had certainly become rosier for me on *DWTS*. After a triumphant Argentine tango that landed me in the top six, and a breakthrough that helped me overcome my crippling anxiety, I headed into the next round of competition free from the pressure that had plagued me for so much of the journey.

Flying High

Unlike so many previous weeks, training went pretty smoothly and our live dances went off without a hitch. To start off, Mark and I were assigned the fox- trot, a ballroom dance in 4/4 time characterized by alternating two slow and two quick steps. We performed to Sam Cooke's "That's It, I Quit, I'm Movin' On," a fun throwback to the 1960s. The whole performance had a vintage feel and the costuming and set made me feel like I was Lucille Ball and Mark was Ricky. Sure, I had some nerves associated with performing a new dance that never went away, but I had a new set of tools to help me through. I breathed deeply, holding my breath for eight counts before exhaling, and repeated that three times. I told myself, "I can do this! I've got this." I remembered that I had access to the choreography that was filed away in my brain. With those tools in place and my newfound confidence, I took the stage with a smile. The enjoyment factor for this dance was huge! I had so much fun and it showed.

Carrie Ann said, "You've had a very difficult struggle the last couple of weeks, like trying to find your footing again, and I can see that you have found your footing. Sometimes it's not about winning, it's about the journey. And what I see is that you have truly made a breakthrough in your mind, in your confidence, in your spirit. And to me, that's 90 percent of what the show is all about. And tonight, you're back on track!"

> Did you know DWTS goes through 4 to 5 gallons of spray tan solution, 20 to 30 bottles of bronzer, and 500 pairs of eyelashes per season?

Whoo hoo! A clear head translated into a great dance. I scored 9s across the board, my best scores of the season up to this point. It was the only dance where I didn't miss a single step. Afterward, Len declared, "It was fun. It was frivolous. It was so joyful to watch. Such a joyful dance." The changes in my heart must have been evident on my face. That's not to say that I had magically become a professional dancer who could memorize routines easily and perform them effortlessly. It was still a lot of hard work to get there physically and mentally on show days! But, I was finally enjoying the ride without the heavy weight that my constant fear of disappointing others had put on me.

In addition to the fox-trot, Mark and I performed a celebrity "dual" dance with Olympic ice dancer Charlie White and his pro partner, Sharna Burgess. The victories I was experiencing mentally freed me to push myself even harder than before. Dancing contemporary to Sam Smith's "Stay with Me," Charlie and I completed a thirty-second lift in the middle of our dance without my feet ever touching the ground. It was a bold and dangerous move. We were the first celebrity couple to ever attempt a lift like that and not even the pro dancers on the show had done a lift lasting as long. With Charlie's strength and experience as an ice dancer, and my comfort and ease with lifts and core strength, we knew we had a winner on our hands. The week felt like a dream.

You may never take the stage in a dance competition. Maybe you'll never have to fox-trot in front of millions, or be hoisted onto the shoulders of an Olympic ice dancer, but the lessons I learned on this journey apply to each of us. That description of fear of man being a snare that we find in the book of Proverbs is so fitting. Whether it's a net, or a noose, or a trick wire, the purpose of a snare is to keep its prey tethered. Fear of man keeps us tethered to worry, doubt, and timidity. When we shed that fear, we are free to leap higher than we ever have before. In my case, I was freed up to leap into the air into a daring and difficult lift. Could we have failed? Sure! And I would have found myself knocked flat in front of a huge audience. But I was suddenly willing to take the risk, because I wasn't just doing this to impress others anymore. I was mentally free to do it for me.

The lifts in that performance were great imagery for how I was feeling that week. Physically, it was a high. I was healthy and happy. Relationally, it was a high. Mark and I were connecting and training well with a new understanding of what made me tick. The camaraderie that I experienced with the other dance teams was energizing, and the love and support from my family, friends, and fans was still pouring in.

But none of that meant that I stopped praying. I was still on my face praying in my trailer every chance I got. I didn't stop reading my Bible. You could find me plopped in the hair and makeup chair with my Bible open when the going was tough *and* when the livin' was easy. That's because the bedrock of my faith is a relationship with Jesus.

In the moments when life is hard and a critical need arises, God is my source of strength. He is the rock I lean on when my own strength fails. In those moments, the Bible is full of life-giving truth that I can cling to. My Christian friends provide prayer and encouragement that helps me go on. But there are also times when there isn't a lot of drama. What does my faith look like then? Much the same as when I'm in crisis mode. During this week of competition when things were going well, I was still asking my prayer team to pray like crazy. I was still praying too! I was still determined to point to Jesus at every opportunity.

This is the arc of the Christian faith. I don't want to be a crisis Christian, who has prayer support and runs to the Word when the house is on fire but lives like I don't need the Lord once the smoke clears. The character of God never changes, and neither does my daily need for Him.

Some churches have a tradition to remind followers of the steadfast goodness of God. It goes like this:

Pastor: God is good . . .

Congregation: All the time!

Pastor: All the time . . .

Congregation: God is good!

I love that! Because we all need the reminder that God's character does not change. He is always, always good. Psalm 100:5 (another psalm of David) says, "For Yahweh is good, and His love is eternal; His faithfulness endures through all generations."

God is good! That's a truth we can take to the bank. God is good when your nerves are shot and you can't remember your next move, and God is good when you perform perfectly and knock it out of the park. The character of God does not change and our need for Him does not change regardless of our circumstances.

Sometimes we can get locked in to wrong patterns of thinking about God. When life is hard we assume that God is mad, and we jump through hoops to try to earn His favor. In contrast, when life is good, we think God must be happy with us. We may default to operating in our own strength as a result. But that's just bad theology. God doesn't change. His love and faithfulness toward us isn't fickle. He is consistent. He models steadfast love for us and then calls us to love Him and love others with the same unflinching dedication.

That's why David wrote, "I will praise the LORD at *all times*; His praise will always be on my lips" (Ps. 34:1, emphasis mine).

God's praises were certainly on my lips at this point in the journey. I was grateful for all that He had carried me through and all that He was continuing to teach me.

In Good Times and In Bad

This pattern of consistency is often modeled for me most tangibly in my closest relationships. I may have gained gobs of Facebook friends and Twitter followers during my *DWTS* run, but my closest friends loved me faithfully before, during, and after this experience. My best friends know me as Candace, not D.J. Tanner on *Full House*, Summer Van Horne on *Make It or Break It*, or celebrity contestant on *DWTS* Season 18.

Yes, I relied heavily on those friendships to smooth out the peaks and valleys of this experience. But real friendship isn't about surviving the roller-coaster ride. My deepest friendships are with people I just do life with. People who have lunch with me when there's not some major life lesson churning in my heart. Friends who are as interested in my life when it's about laundry and carpools and grocery shopping as

when it's about red-carpet walks and high-profile opportunities. Most of these friendships I've had since high school, like
my best friend, Dilini, whom I met in tenth grade. We've
spent countless nights in our sweatpants with frizzy hair and
no makeup talking on the couch about everything to nothing at all. We can sit in comfortable silence or listen to one
another talk each other's ear off when life is pressing.

In fact, this journey helped me treasure those relationships that are well oiled with years of the mundane. I
couldn't have survived much of the emotional turmoil that
came with being on *DWTS* without my friends and family,
but I need them just as much to survive and thrive in "normal" life.

That's especially true in my marriage. Just like I seek to
have a consistent relationship with Jesus, I want to nurture a
solid marriage at *all* times. I don't only spend time with my
husband when the road is rocky and we need each other for
support. We vowed to love each other in good times too!

Yes, Val was a hero during this experience. He made
breakfasts, packed lunches, shuffled boys to hockey practice
and Natasha to tennis matches, double-checked homework,
and made dinners every night—all while cheering me on
from the sidelines. He was a wise advisor, faithful encourager,
and proactive partner for every single step of my *DWTS* journey. But that's nothing new. That's the kind of husband he is
and the kind of wife I strive to be.

This picture of marriage was beautifully illustrated by
Mark in an interview we did after *DWTS* wrapped. Mark was
appearing on *Huff Post LIVE* and I popped into the studio to
surprise him as a guest host. Hoping for an inside scoop on
his formative years, I asked him, "What's the greatest lesson
that your mom and dad taught you about being a partner?"

(Note: Mark's parents are competitive ballroom dancers, Corky and Shirley Ballas.)

His answer blew me away.

"My mom and dad were legendary ballroom dancers. From them, it's just really being there 100 percent for your partner. As a man, you have to be the frame. The woman is the art. When you take a dance, Paso, for instance. The man is the matador and the woman represents the cape. You have to be in command. You have to be protective and nurturing but a strong spirit for your partner at all times. Even though you are doing your moves, you have to keep an eye on your partner all the time to make sure that she's okay and to make sure that she is flourishing on the end of your arm. And I think my dad was such an amazing role model in that sense for my mom, because my mom was and still is one of the best female Latin dancers to ever grace the floor, and without a great partner you can't be an amazing female dancer."[12]

Don't you just love that description? Val is my frame. And whether or not I am "flourishing" depends, in part, on his consistent love and support. Marriages aren't made up of honeymoons and date nights. Almost two decades after saying "I do," I can tell you there's a lot of mundane in between the peaks and valleys. But that is where the good stuff really happens. I am so grateful for Val's support as I took on this huge challenge on a massive stage, but I am equally grateful for his support as I face the tasks of parenting, running a household, and finding purpose in life's many routines.

The arc of my deepest relationships mirrors the arc of my walk with Christ. Yes, there are times of crisis when I need those relationships desperately. There are also times of great joy when the people I love most are a natural part of the celebration. But there are times when life is just life, the road is smooth, and the scenery is nothing special. I still need Jesus then. I still need friendship then. I still need family then.

As week eight wrapped, the end of the roller-coaster ride was in sight. I wanted to cross that finish line so badly now with a mirrorball trophy at arm's length. But for so many reasons, I was looking forward to normal, in all the ways that mattered most. My life was the same on and off the *DWTS* stage. God's goodness was a constant; so were my most important relationships.

By now, I'm sure my love for the Lord is pretty clear, but do you know *why* my relationship with Jesus is so important? You hear about people finding God when they've come into crisis or hit rock-bottom. There's nothing left and they have no hope, so they find hope in God. But what about someone like me, who had everything going for her and never really hit any major roadblocks? Life has been good! Is that you? You've got a job, maybe a family and good friends, you're happy and most of all, consider yourself a good person? Have you ever wondered why you'd need Jesus if life looks perfectly good the way you're living it?

For me, the gospel moved from my head to my heart when I realized that even though I was a "good girl" living a "good life" when I used others as my measuring stick, compared to the blinding white of God's holiness, my goodness looked like a pile of dirty rags.

Romans 3:10 says, "There is no one righteous, not even one."

Righteousness is a churchy word for being free from sin. When we hold ourselves up to the perfect, holy nature of

God, it's easy to see that we can't measure up. I'm sure you've heard of the Ten Commandments, the rules for living that God handed down to Moses for the people of Israel in Exodus 20. Sure, I look like a good girl when I consider some of God's rules. I've never murdered. I've never stolen. But what about lying? Gulp. How about that commandment not to want something someone else has (the Bible calls that coveting)? Guilty. How about His commandment that I have no other gods beside Him? I've been guilty of idolatry before, worshipping comfort, or security, or acceptance instead of God. But, I've only broken three commandments so far. I've still kept 70 percent. That's passing!

But . . .

"For whoever keeps the entire law, yet fails in one point, is guilty of breaking it all" (James 2:10).

Double gulp!

Since I am guilty of breaking *some* of God's law, the Bible says I am guilty of breaking *all* of it.

All of us have failed to meet God's standards. That's called sin. And no matter how hard we try, we cannot stop sinning on our own. Sin nature is an unfortunate and irreversible part of humanity.

Romans 3:23 puts it this way, "For all have sinned and fall short of the glory of God."

It doesn't matter if you were valedictorian or a high school dropout, if you have a rap sheet a mile long or have never even had a speeding ticket. It doesn't matter if others see you as a bad girl or a good girl. Every one of us is a sinner who misses God's mark.

When I finally saw myself as a sinner, in need of grace from a sinless God, suddenly I understood the gospel. All of my clean living couldn't earn me a place in heaven because it didn't make up for the fact that I am a sinner, and I can't stop sinning.

That's the bad news, but there is good news.

Jesus died to pay the penalty for my sins. He paid the price that I could never pay. It's kind of like breaking the law and not having the money to pay your fine. If you can't pay, you have to serve your time. But just before you head off to a life of imprisonment, a man shows up with money and pays your debt for you, not wanting anything in return. He does it out of love for you, to free you from the punishment you should have paid yourself. That's exactly what Jesus did for you and for me. And He didn't stop there! When I realized my desperate need for Him and surrendered my life for Him, He began a miraculous work of transformation in me. Every day, He is making me more like Him. He's not making me a better version of a good girl. He is making me a holy version of a good girl. Someone who thinks, acts, and lives more and more like Him because of His work in me. And the Bible promises that He will continue to mold and shape my heart until I am complete and can stand before Him holy and blameless.

It's this constant molding and shaping that makes me a person of conviction. This is what informs my decisions about what is right and appropriate for me as a Christian woman. At the very beginning of this book, I told you that my convictions were set before I ever received the offer to be on *DWTS*. Those kinds of life decisions shouldn't be made in the heat of the moment or in the valleys. They are made in the constant, day in and day out, walking with the Lord. He guides and leads every day and when the going gets tough, our convictions are set and He's there to pull us through.

And what a wonderful testimony to a watching world! When we as Christians move through this life leaning on

Him, in good times and bad, becoming more and more like Christ, we point others to Him all along the way.

"But now He has reconciled you by His physical body through His death, to present you holy, faultless, and blameless before Him" (Col. 1:22).

As you face the peaks and valleys of life, I hope you know where to look for your "frame." God will love you well and shore you up no matter what you face in life because He paid the ultimate price for our sin, reconciling us to God and promising us the fruit of the Spirit—love, joy, peace, patience, goodness, kindness, gentleness, faithfulness, and self-control—along with all His strength at all times in our lives, not just during our difficult circumstances. David knew that lesson well. He ran to God when the going was tough and when the living was easy. No matter where you are on that spectrum right now, you can lean in to Jesus. May His praise be ever on your lips.

> I will praise the LORD at all times;
> His praise will always be on my lips.
> I will boast in the LORD;
> the humble will hear and be glad. (Ps. 34:1–2)

Chapter 10

Fix My Eyes

But my eyes look to You, Lord GOD.
I seek refuge in You; do not let me die.
—PSALM 141:8

Who is your hero?

Did you know the Bible actually gives us the qualifications for heroes? It's true! Hebrews 11:1–2 says, "Now faith is the reality of what is hoped for, the proof of what is not seen. For our ancestors won God's approval by it."

That passage goes on to applaud the superheroes of the faith like Abraham, Moses, David, and Samuel. These spiritual giants didn't possess extraordinary talents or supernatural abilities. It was their faith that made them strong! They are the superstars of the Bible because they trusted and obeyed the Lord.

It was the semifinals and week nine of my *DWTS* journey was Icon Week. Each remaining celebrity was asked to choose one of their heroes to be interviewed for the show. While others selected TV personalities, record executives, or Olympic athletes, I knew I wanted to pick a Bible teacher as my icon. I'll admit it's exciting to rub shoulders with celebrities, but it doesn't compare to the thrill I get from connecting with my favorite Bible teachers and pastors. Through their speaking and studies, Bible teachers have had a huge influence in my life. They genuinely excite me more than any celebrity. Because of that, I selected Angela Thomas to be my icon for the show. Angela is a Bible teacher, speaker, and best-selling author of many books and Bible studies. We met at a series of Extraordinary Women conferences. As we worked together at events over the years, Angela became a friend and a mentor.

I knew that Angela had been watching the show every week. She sweetly let me know that she and her family had been getting together faithfully every Monday night to watch, and I was absolutely tickled to death that she was rooting for me. Her support was particularly encouraging because I admire her so much, but also because within the Christian community there were still some Bible teachers who questioned my decision to be on the show. As the weeks went on and I proved that it was possible to be on *DWTS* and stand with conviction, more and more Christian voices lent their support, but Angela had been cheering me on since the beginning. I wanted the whole world to know that her faith inspired and encouraged me.

I reached out to Angela and asked her if she could fly in to be interviewed for the show. Here's a snapshot of our text conversations:

Me: Hey Angela!! SO, this week on *DWTS* is Icon Week and I have to choose my personal icon or influencer and I really want a Bible teacher. Is there any chance you're available today, tomorrow, or Sunday to fly in for an interview with me for the show? The notice is crazy short, so sorry.

Angela: I am so humbled. And honored. YES. I can come! Just landed in Minneapolis to speak. Can't come until Sunday if that works for you.

Angela later said that she thought I had sent her that text by mistake and considered sending me a list of "big name" people to invite instead. That made me giggle.

It's true that my icon didn't have the star power that some of the other contestants tapped into. Amy Purdy called Oprah Winfrey. You can't find a bigger name than that. James Maslow asked for legendary record producer L. A. Reid. Charlie and Meryl called on fellow Olympic champions Scott Hamilton and Kristi Yamaguchi. There's just something about star power that makes people "ooh" and "ah," so the producers and my team of managers started pushing me toward someone with celebrity status even though I had already asked Angela. I was convinced in my heart that Angela was the right person for the job, but I allowed them to come up with alternative names to investigate to satisfy them. They sent out a request to a handful of celebrities to be on the show, but the time line was too short and none of the alternates were available for an interview. It didn't surprise me one bit when those doors closed. I knew it was a God thing and was relieved. Angela was the one I wanted; I knew she was the perfect person to represent my personal icon.

Her response to the whole thing was precious. She proved to be the woman of faith that I admired so much.

Angela: This is the craziest, most fun change of plans ever. Thank you for inviting me to come. I've wanted to text you a thousand times because I have been bursting with pride. So very blessed each week to watch you shine. And especially God in you!

Me: Xoxoxo. Can't wait!!

In no time, Angela joined me in L.A. Our interview together was such an encouragement and blessing. They also interviewed Angela alone, asking her questions about me and my journey and what she thought about all of it. The producers chose the song "Nasty" by Janet Jackson for me to dance to that week and they tried to corner Angela on it a time or two with questions like, "Candace has the song 'Nasty.' What do you think God would say about that?"

Angela just refused to go there or give them a sound bite that could be misunderstood. She never wavered in her support of me and her commitment to point people to Jesus. She humbly and graciously acknowledged that she wasn't the real icon that week. Jesus is my icon. Angela knew that and her graciousness and reassurance was a priceless gift.

She continued to pray for me and send me Scripture for the remainder of my journey. Here's a taste of what happened after the cameras stopped rolling:

Me: Angela, I hope your flight back home was good! Just wanted to say another thank-you for not only your willingness to fly here on such short notice and be a part of my DWTS journey package, but for all your encouragement, support, wisdom, and AWESOME cheerleading skills! You're the best. Your enthusiasm for me made me feel so special, and as fun as this journey is, it's been exhausting

and such a spiritual battle and difficult on numerous levels.
Thank you for coming up alongside me any time I've asked
you. You are such a valuable, dear friend and mentor to me.
I love you. Xo.

Angela: With all my heart, I believe this will be your most
confident week of dancing yet! Nobody predicted this.
Not Mark. Not the DWTS producers. But when God is for
you, who in this world can be against you? The answer is,
though they try, no one is bigger than your God. He will do
as He wills. I hope you and Mark are having a blast. I'm
praying that even the hardest technique moments are filled
with joy and a spirit of celebration.

Unbelievably, the semifinal show kicked off with my video
package with Angela. God's name was declared and glorified
at the very start of the show! In the end I was so grateful to
have the opportunity to showcase one of my true heroes. She
may not have many red-carpet walks under her belt, but she's
a superstar in my book because she loves Jesus with her whole
heart and serves Him with her whole life. Angela was the
perfect pick because I knew and trusted her and there was an
intimacy between us that was unique. She brought me back
to reality and reminded me:

- This is who I really am.
- This is who I look up to.
- My role models are people who are running the race
  of faith with reckless abandon.

Angela continued to encourage me and point me to Jesus for the last leg of the journey. Her steady drip of praise and truth meant so much to me! I know I'm not the only one who has been inspired and strengthened by her words. They matter for all of us who desire to earn our commendation through faith. Here's one more snapshot of her wisdom:

> **Angela:** You've done it. All. The. Way. You have done every hard thing with integrity and grace. God's assignment to you means one last night to give a blessing to everyone you speak to. Grips. Stylists. Judges. Mark. No Christian has done this show with the same spirit of faithfulness to God. You've taught us all how to shine in the dark. How to love even when others are unloving. We all pray that when the time comes, we will act and respond like Jesus. This was your time and you radiate the beauty and joy of Christ!! I speak for so many who are bursting with pride over you . . . Savor. Enjoy. Celebrate. I love you and cheer wildly for you. He chose brilliantly when He chose you!

A Smile That Wouldn't Stick

My time with Angela was one of the highlights of my *DWTS* experience, but like so much of the journey, that week was bittersweet.

At this point in the show, we were learning two full dances each week. Mark and I were assigned to do the waltz, a dance in triple time characterized by rhythmic turns around the dance floor. Our second routine was a jazz dance. At this point in the contest, couples were allowed to practice up to twelve hours per day, seven days a week. Mark and I were the only couple using all of our hours, because I needed the

practice. I picked up the waltz easily. I had the routine down
in a single day. We had a flawless dress rehearsal. It felt like a
no-brainer routine. I had this one!

The jazz didn't go so smoothly. Since the song "Nasty"
was selected for us, I knew that might ruffle some feathers, but I really wasn't stressed about it. I was gaining some
ground in not being afraid of those who seemed determined
to criticize the song or my wardrobe choices. Plus, Janet
Jackson was one of my favorite artists growing up. No doubt,
she's fun to dance to. For me, the stress was tied to the type
of routine Mark choreographed. Mark was strategic. When
he heard our song choice, he said up front that he did not
want to do a dance that looked like a Janet Jackson video.
He wanted to do a classic jazz routine, more like what you'd
see in Broadway theater productions like *Chicago* than you
would see on MTV. He was trying to protect me from being
put in a compromising position with moves that were overtly
sexual. Because of that, Mark developed a routine where he
and I would dance side by side. There was hardly any connection between us on the dance floor so if I messed up, it would
be obvious. There wasn't any place for Mark to get me back
on track. I had a history of needing him to help me course-
correct during each live performance. He had stepped in and
saved me in every previous dance except the fox-trot. As we
practiced, I started to panic because, ultimately, I was learning to do a solo routine to be performed beside a professional
dancer. I knew that every mistake would be noticeable.

During rehearsals I started to get very frustrated and
upset. I told Mark I needed a break and gave him every excuse
I could think of for why my attitude was deteriorating and I
couldn't learn the steps.

While Mark had a history of being an empathetic teacher, his tone was different this time around.

He said, "I understand that you are frustrated, but this is what you have to do. Your attitude is so bad. You're bringing everything down. You're not learning this routine *because* of your attitude."

His words felt like a punch to the gut because I knew he was right. I promised I would try to turn my attitude around, but I just couldn't do it. At one point, I was just beyond myself. I couldn't get the steps right. I messed up in different places every time, so it wasn't like there was a specific stumbling block that Mark could address and correct. I was so discouraged. I was visibly frustrated and down on myself. Mark was done trying to give me any pep talks. Understandably, he was frustrated too and he simply ran out of peppy words.

I'm sure you've been there. For whatever reason, you just can't talk yourself out of your funk. The people around you have run out of inspiration and you feel stuck. What then? I did the only thing I knew to do. I stopped, right in the middle of the routine. I took my microphone off and I went and hid in a closet.

If you watched the show, you might be wondering if you missed this scene, but the inside scoop is that none of it was caught on camera. In fact, I don't believe it would have happened if the cameras had been rolling. I literally hid in a closet to escape the cameras because I needed to get out of my headspace. I needed a radical change of scenery so I could step into the ring and wrestle with my out-of-control emotions.

Inside the closet I tried to pump myself up. I tried to plaster on a smile like I had in week three, but no matter how hard I tried, I could not get that smile to stick. The happy chemicals in my brain were overwhelmed by the frustration and self-doubt I was feeling. I just couldn't seem to force myself to get happy. I prayed my heart out. I said, "God, I am asking for Your help to get out of this funk. I don't know what to do. I cannot figure this out and I need it to stop."

Eventually the producers found me. I begged them not to send in the camera. I told them I needed a few more minutes. They graciously agreed. I took a deep breath and walked back into the rehearsal studio. But I knew nothing had changed. My attitude still stunk!

At that point I was so irritated by being inside my own body. I wanted out of myself but I was stuck with me. (Please tell me you've felt like this before!) I asked the producers for five minutes with Mark with no cameras. They reluctantly agreed and I motioned for Mark to step into the hallway with me. Mark said later than when I motioned to him to speak privately, he braced himself to hear me say I was quitting. But that's not what I said. Instead, I looked Mark straight in the eyes and said as seriously as he'd ever seen me, "I need you to help me. My attitude sucks! I can't even stand to be within myself right now. I don't want to be around myself, but I can't shake it. I recognize it's totally me. You've been extremely patient. You've been a great teacher."

In that moment I had several options. I could have quit, like Mark expected me to. When the going got really tough, I could have simply taken off my dance shoes and gone home. But I would have forfeited my chance to cross the finish line. I was too close to let that happen now. I could have exploded, venting to Mark about why this routine was so hard and why the choreography was too tough and that my frustration was feeding off his frustration with me and voicing every excuse I could think of. But that would have just thrown fuel on the fire that was already raging inside of me and put Mark in an even more uncomfortable and aggravated position. Instead, I chose a more difficult path—a path my flesh resisted every step of the way. I chose repentance, owning up to the ways my sin was wreaking havoc and I chose to ask for help.

Of course repentance is God's idea. It comes straight from His Word.

James 5:16 says, "Therefore, confess your sins to one another and pray for one another, so that you may be healed. The urgent request of a righteous person is very powerful in its effect."

We don't need a mediator between God and us. We are free to confess our sins to Him at any time and He is ready and willing to forgive us, but there is power in dragging our sins out into the light. I had already taken my frustration and anxiety to God in the closet, but now I needed to confess them to Mark. After all, he had been impacted by my behavior and he was uniquely positioned to provide accountability moving forward.

> There were probably some "dudes" peppered in this conversation. Mark and I call each other "dude" more than our actual names.

As we talked, my need to repent in other areas became obvious. At one point I had told Mark in exasperation that I hated the dance he created. He told me that he was really hurt over my words and found them rude. He had worked extremely hard to create the routine and felt unappreciated and disrespected. He was right. Instead of defending myself, I simply said, "I'm sorry." It was rude. Truth be told, I didn't really hate the routine, I just hated the way I was having trouble learning and performing it in that moment.

Ultimately, repentance was what flipped the switch for me. It was like the fog lifted and I felt so much better. We walked back into the studio, performed the routine, and the producers stopped us and said, "What just happened?" The difference was evident. I knew that moment could not have happened with the cameras rolling. I needed to privately deal with my own sin and then go to the person I had sinned against one-on-one, without millions of people watching.

That became a defining moment for me and for Mark. I learned the power of humble repentance. I can understand why James tied public confession to powerful prayer in the verse I mentioned above. I needed to get real about my sin to make room for God to move. And He did! I was able to practice and learn the routine without the panic and frustration that had seemed chained to me just a few minutes earlier. And Mark had been able to complete a missing piece of choreography that also had him stuck.

In the end, we performed a dance that guest judge Kenny Ortega—a three-time Emmy-winning director and choreographer—pronounced "brilliant," saying I reminded him of the great ladies of Broadway. Len said, "There was nothing nasty about that. It was crisp, it was clean, it was tight, and it was together. Well done!" We scored two 9s and two perfect 10s. It was our highest scores of the entire season and I felt like we killed it! I have no doubt things would have turned out very differently if instead of repenting and asking for help, I had dug in or walked away during that difficult rehearsal.

A Waltz Gone Wrong

With all of the drama that surrounded our jazz number, I expected the waltz to go off without a hitch. I had learned it easily in practice and loved every part of our routine to Bruno Mars's song "If I Knew." My peach-jeweled floral corset top and long skirt was feminine and old-fashioned, and I felt more beautiful than ever in it. As Mark and I prepared to take the stage, I felt comfortable and confident. But things didn't exactly go as planned.

After the first quarter of the routine, I was supposed to do a turn where Mark then dipped me in his arms. But after the spin I blanked and hesitated. Mark quickly got me into the dip but when I came up, I didn't know where I was in the routine. My eyes were like saucers and Mark saw the confusion on my face. He whispered my next steps and I quickly adjusted my arms and feet and we kept dancing. Just a few steps later, I did the wrong move again and mistakenly placed my arm around Mark's shoulder. He moved my arm back in front of him into the proper hold and we kept dancing, but he knew mentally, I was done. I had made too many mistakes in too short of a time span and I couldn't recover. He started whispering every move into my ear . . .

> We weren't allowed to keep our costumes, but we had the option to purchase them. I bought five; the quickstep two-piece rocker, the Little Mermaid samba two-piece, the silver blingy cha-cha-cha dress, the purple and black Argentine tango dress, and the old-fashioned peach Viennese waltz dress. I wish I could have bought all of them, but they were quite pricey!

"I got you. Left foot. Right foot. We're about to turn here . . ."

He talked me through every single step. I was so disappointed in myself and upset after the dance because I felt like

I had blown it. Before we took the stage, Mark had predicted we would get 10s because I knew this routine so well. Instead, we ended up with two 8s and two 9s.

God had taken a routine that was challenging for me and turned it into a lesson about repentance. He truly is able to make beauty from ashes. Romans 8:28 promises that He works everything for our good. My perfect waltz gone wrong was no exception. A friend of mine, Karen Ehman, wrote about that dance on her blog. She's an accomplished writer, but her post titled "What Candace Cameron Bure's Waltz Teaches Us about God" became one of her most shared posts ever.

I wept when I read the post for the first time because her words helped me think beyond the dance floor. I wanted to pass them along to you . . .

> This season on *Dancing with the Stars* . . . Candace Cameron Bure is a participant. Since she and I have become friends in the past few years by speaking at conferences and doing online ministry together, I have followed the show this season. Okay. More than followed. I've become a totally obsessed fan. Haven't missed an episode.
>
> I get updates from Candace about how rehearsal is going. This past week I knew she was dancing a Viennese waltz and then a jazz number. When she and partner Mark Ballas took the floor to perform their waltz, I put down my pita chips and hummus and riveted my eyes to the screen.
>
> She looked gorgeous. And elegant. The dance started out well. But then a slight misstep caused her to momentarily lose her place.

She continued on. It became evident that Mark was speaking to her as they whirled and twirled around the dance floor in sync, attempting to complete the number.

When the song ended and they made their way over to chat with the show's host Tom Bergeron, Candace was visibly upset with herself. The judges pointed out that she indeed had momentarily lost her place but that they were proud of the fact that she kept on dancing.

After the judges' comments on the number and before they revealed their scores, Tom asked Mark a question. He wanted to know what he was saying to Candace as they were waltzing their way to the end of the routine. Mark replied, "I've got you. It's okay. Right leg. Left leg. Stretch. Turn around. I've got you. It's okay. Love you. Love you. Love you. We're gonna make it. We're gonna make it."

I know this chant of encouragement was for Candace during the dance, but later that evening, I couldn't get Mark's words off my mind.

When immersed in the great dance of life, sometimes I forget my place. My feet get tangled. My mind goes blank. Bewildered, I continue on, although I'm totally uncertain of what to do next.

While I rehearse life's scenarios over and over again, surmising just how they will turn out once the music starts, sometimes life's dance doesn't always go just as planned. I'm guessing it is the same with you at times. Maybe?

We vow to have a loving and loyal marriage, but then

domestic disputes happen. We say and do things that we had not intended. Our marriage drifts off course and we aren't sure what to do to get back in step with our spouse.

We purpose to be an intentional parent. To raise our children to be loving and respectful. Children that would make any parent proud. But then one of them makes a bad choice. A *really* bad choice. So we beat ourselves up emotionally over and over again, wrongly surmising that we are our child's choices. Though the music keeps blaring, we can't seem to put one foot in front of the other. We are just too discouraged with our poor parenting skills.

Or maybe we ourselves choose poorly. Irrationally. Even immorally. We want to stop the conductor and abandon the dance. We've messed up far too much to go on.

It is then that the Lord gently takes our hand, pulls us in close and with loving reassurance whispers sweetly to our soul . . .

"I've got you. It's okay."

But Lord. I just can't . . .

"Yes you can. Follow Me now. Right leg. Left leg."

But I've messed up big time . . .

"Stretch."

Lord, that stretch hurt . . .

"Yes it did. Now turn around."

You mean repent?

"Yes. I've got you. I've got you. It's okay. I love you. Just keep your eyes on Me. Listen only to My voice. Follow Me:

I. Love. You."

When it came time for Mark and Candace's second dance, she danced with a confidence that earned her and Mark their best scores of the season including two perfect 10s. All because she forgot her past, changed her ways, and allowed her teacher to get her back on course.

As we waltz through life and something happens to cause us to stumble, it is never too late to listen to the Master's loving words to us as He gently and graciously consoles, corrects, and restores.

Can you hear Him now? He is gently whispering to you . . .

"We're gonna make it. We're gonna make it. Just keep listening to Me, My love, and . . .

Dance on."

". . . and that you may love the LORD your God, listen to his voice, and hold fast to him. For the LORD is your life . . . " (Deut. 30:20 NIV)[13]

Chapter 11

Crossing the Finish Line

Therefore, since we also have such a large cloud of witnesses surrounding us, let us lay aside every weight and the sin that so easily ensnares us. Let us run with endurance the race that lies before us.
—HEBREWS 12:1

Cliff Young knew how to finish a race.

In 1983, Cliff won the Westfield Sydney to Melbourne Ultramarathon. He ran from Sydney to Melbourne, Australia, a distance of almost 550 miles in a record-breaking time of five days, fifteen hours, and four minutes. He beat the previous record by almost two days.

The crazy thing about Cliff is that he was not a marathon runner. In fact, he'd never run in a single race before. Cliff was not an athlete. He was a potato farmer. He wasn't young. Remarkably, he crossed the finish line at the age of sixty-one. His training had been in the sheep fields. After the race, he told reporters that while he was running he imagined that he was chasing sheep and trying to outrun a storm. Most of the other runners had big-name sponsors like Nike and high-tech running gear to prove it. Cliff showed up for the race in his overalls and work boots.

There's never been a more likeable underdog than Cliff. When he won, he divvied up the $10,000 in prize money among the other five racers who finished the race. He didn't keep a penny for himself. The following year he entered another race and was awarded a Mitsubishi Colt for his courage. He instantly deferred to the tenacity of a competitor and gave the keys to the other runner. Cliff Young never kept a single prize, but he kept running into his eighties.[14]

When asked what drives him, Cliff once told a magazine reporter, "I like to finish what I start doing. I like to see it through to the end, to the best of my ability."[15]

Cliff was not a marathon runner, but that didn't keep him out of the race. I am not a ballroom dancer, but that didn't keep me off the *DWTS* stage. As I was pushed through to the final four by my incredible fan support and rounded the corner of week ten of my *DWTS* journey, the finish line was in sight, but the last leg of the race is often the hardest. I had to dig deep to get through. But this wasn't about dancing anymore. It wasn't about a mirrorball trophy or ratings. I wanted to see this baby through to the end. I was determined to do so to the best of my abilities.

Man Down!

As rehearsals began for week ten, only four of us remained. Mark and I were assigned two dances, the quickstep and a freestyle.

Each couple was required to return to the style of dance they did during switch-up week. I did the quickstep with Tony and now it was time to do it again with Mark. At this stage in the game, all of the competitors were beyond exhausted. The competition was less like a marathon and more like an eleven-week-long sprint when you count our rehearsals before the show ever started. We were winded and wrung out but we simply had to press through.

I struggled to master the quickstep, even though I had already performed it once. It should have come easier to me the second time around, but the switch-up had been six weeks prior, I'd learned a lot of steps in the meantime, and I was mentally and physically exhausted.

For our freestyle, Mark and I chose to disco. Mark really wanted to knock it out of the park so instead of doing a type of dance the audience had already seen me do before, like contemporary, he wanted something fun, fresh, and exciting that would really get them pumped watching. Through his

Training for *DWTS* was very physically demanding. I did not work out or lift weights in addition to dancing while on the show because I was already pushing my body to the max. I only lost a total of four pounds while on the show, but I leaned out and lost several inches. By week four, I had to increase my calories so I wouldn't lose any more weight and become too thin.

years of experience on the show, Mark felt it was the freestyle that ultimately won or lost you the competition.

"This is the dance that makes you amazing or breaks you!" he told me.

We chose the song "Canned Heat" by Jamiroquai. You might know it best from the movie *Napoleon Dynamite*. (Gosh!) I love that movie so we thought it would be a fun pick. Our costumes were all solid gold and over-the-top silly and we had a D.J. Candyball theme in honor of D.J. Tanner. We thought we had all of the elements for a killer performance the audience and judges would love.

Rehearsals were extra challenging because of the exhaustion factor. There was one point on Sunday morning before camera blocking, but still at the rehearsal studio, where Mark kept pushing the side of my neck and face back to get me into the proper frame for our quickstep. After one push a little too hard, I lost it and started crying and walked out of the studio. That scene was all caught on camera of course and ended up being in my video package for the live show. Lots of people expressed frustration with Mark after that show aired, but he wasn't acting aggressively toward me. He had done the same thing many times before using an arm's-length technique to get his partner back into frame, although in his frustration, he pushed a little quicker and harder than normal and at that point I was so tired and oversensitive that I couldn't handle it. "Dude, you're being so dramatic right now," Mark said. I was, but it was all very real. It was an extremely stressful week because we wanted the dances to be perfect but we were both coasting on fumes.

In that situation, the show was an endurance game. All of the couples were struggling under the weight of the ongoing stress and strain on our bodies. The race became about survival of the fittest, and injuries were happening left and right. Unfortunately, we weren't immune. During that same day, just one day before the live show, Mark tore his rotator cuff as we were camera blocking our freestyle routine in the middle of our first lift. As he was whisked off to the emergency room, I started to freak out. The producers informed me that they didn't know if Mark would be able to dance and assigned me Artem Chigvintev, one of the troupe dancers, as my new partner. Mark and I had been working together for eleven weeks at this point. We were one day away from the finals and suddenly I was on a whole new team.

> Some of the troupe dancers have been pros on shows like *DWTS* in other countries. Artem won Season 8 with his celeb partner on *Strictly Come Dancing*. Artem returned to *DWTS* as a pro in Season 19 with Lea Thompson.

It couldn't have happened on a worse day. It was the most minute-by-minute scheduled day of the entire season. We were supposed to be practicing and camera blocking in between interviews with all of the major media outlets. The schedule looked something like this . . .

12:03 makeup and hair touch-ups
12:08 *Good Morning America* interview
12:26 camera block 1st dance
12:48 *Access Hollywood* interview
1:00 *Entertainment Tonight* interview
1:12 wardrobe fitting
1:28 social media video
1:35 weekly magazine interviews

1:50 camera block 2nd dance

2:12 *DWTS* package interview

This intense schedule continued until 6:00 p.m., where I then needed to get my ever-famous spray tan and continue practicing back at the rehearsal studio until 11:00 p.m.

I was so frazzled by the stress and exhaustion. Mark and I were at each other's throats because we were so tired and then suddenly, my partner was lying on the floor kicking his feet and crying out in pain. There was nothing in me that felt like going on. Every cell in my body screamed, "I can't do this!" but I had already learned the secret to pushing through. Yes, I was weak. Yes, I was at the end of my rope. But that is where God's office is. His power is perfected in my weakness. When I'm spent, He's just getting warmed up.

I knew I wasn't really running this race to win a mirror-ball. This was about standing with conviction. This was about showcasing the grace and joy that God had given to me. This was about having courage in the face of opposition, whether that opposition came from others or from my own insecurities. This was about seizing every opportunity to live for God's glory.

> One of my refuges was a Russian-style spa I often visited after practices. I'd alternate from hot tub to cold tub (brrrrr!) and the banya (a Russian sauna).

I wanted to be like the potato-farmer-turned-marathon-runner, Cliff Young. I wanted to cross that finish line, not to grab a victory for myself but so I could "toss the keys" to the Author and Perfecter of my faith.

Hebrews 12:1–2 says it this way:

Therefore, since we also have such a large cloud of witnesses surrounding us, let us lay aside every weight and the sin that so easily ensnares us. Let us run with endurance the race that lies before us, keeping our eyes on Jesus, the source and perfecter of our faith, who for the joy that lay before Him endured a cross and despised the shame and has sat down at the right hand of God's throne.

I was surrounded by a great cloud of witnesses all right. Millions were watching to see how I would finish this race. I wanted to throw off the stress and exhaustion and frustration and run with endurance.

Still Standing

The producers stepped in and immediately started problem-solving, reworking my schedule and situation as best as possible. They canceled my press interviews and rushed me back to the rehearsal studio with Artem and Cheryl Burke after making sure I had a few bites of food for energy before starting in again. Artem was learning both dances from watching our previously taped rehearsal video while he simultaneously rehearsed them with me. Cheryl, a professional dancer who had already been eliminated, was assigned to stay with me and help me with the transition, particularly in the mental department for encouragement.

Learning the dances with a new partner felt so different, but Artem was a total pro, making it as comfortable and seamless as possible. Aside from that, I hadn't nailed down my quickstep with Mark, and never actually completed a full run of it during camera blocking so I was still trying to learn and memorize it. Artem talked and danced me through everything with his Russian accent and masculine sense of control and calmness over the situation that felt familiar from the years with my husband. Cheryl had an easy and relaxed, this-won't-be-a-problem kind of smile on her face while she helped me learn the techniques from a female perspective. Cheryl even called in for a new style of ballroom heels to be sent over immediately for me because she knew they would be more comfortable and stable, helping me with the flow of the movements. And they were! Cheryl and Artem's support was invaluable.

Monday rolled around and it was time for dress rehearsal. Mark had left the hospital after his initial visit to the ER, but had to return the following day for an MRI. I still didn't know the extent of his injuries or if he and I would dance together on the live show.

Artem and I camera blocked the dances on stage that morning and then Mark returned to the set. He had a small tear in his shoulder, but the doctors had cleared him to dance. The producers were still leery and so was I. I didn't want to be the reason that Mark had permanent damage to his shoulder. I knew how much was at stake since Mark was a professional dancer and I certainly didn't want him making any rash decisions for the sake of TV or a possible trophy. It wasn't worth it.

The doctors, producers, Mark, and I all agreed that if Mark could get through the dress rehearsal without any problems and I felt at complete ease that I wouldn't be in fear of hurting him again, he could do the live show. If anything happened during those two hours, Artem would be taking his place. We started to practice and Mark realized that some of the lifts would put too much strain on his injured body.

He was literally changing the choreography seconds before we performed in our dress rehearsal. I'd had a hard enough time learning everything to begin with, and now the dance was in flux.

Mark was approved for the live show and with all of those factors in play, we went out and did the very best quickstep and freestyle we could. I had a blast and I felt like Mark and I danced as well as we could, particularly under the circumstances. We scored three 9s for our quickstep, which was good considering I once again missed a few steps. I was disappointed, however, to score three 8s on the freestyle, which I had so much fun doing and honestly thought went really well. The judges didn't agree, saying that although I went for it and my tenacity was admired, I didn't quite connect with the music and my timing was a millisecond off beat. I didn't fully agree with the judges this time, but I knew a debate wasn't the right choice. I told Erin Andrews, the cohost, during her post-dance interview that I had a lot of fun and hoped the audience had as much fun watching as I did performing. It was my way of politely shaking off what they said.

After we all danced, it was time for the final elimination. James Maslow's name was called and I was left standing between two Olympic athletes, Meryl Davis and Amy Purdy.

Even though we still had the finale show to go through the very next night, I felt like I had already won. I had far exceeded my own personal goals and expectations for the show and I had

I'm the only person who made it to the finals who did not receive a perfect score at any point in the competition. I was a true underdog! My fans pushed me into the final three!

pushed through fears, frustrations, pain, and roadblocks. I felt like fist-pumping and shouting out a "Whoop! Whoop!" I had pushed myself further than I ever thought I could and I felt like I'd already crossed the finish line.

Paul must have known a thing or two about difficult races.

In 1 Corinthians 9:24–27 he writes:

> Don't you know that the runners in a stadium all race, but only one receives the prize? Run in such a way to win the prize. Now everyone who competes exercises self-control in everything. However, they do it to receive a crown that will fade away, but we a crown that will never fade away. Therefore I do not run like one who runs aimlessly or box like one beating the air. Instead, I discipline my body and bring it under strict control, so that after preaching to others, I myself will not be disqualified.

Paul points out an obvious reality. Competitive runners all run the race knowing that only one of them can win first place. Since there can be only one first-place winner, perhaps it's not the medal or crown that matters most, but how we run the race. Paul encourages us not to be aimless (v. 26), like a boxer beating the air, but to run with purpose, keeping the prize at the forefront of our minds.

Paul wasn't talking about marathon running here. The race is our lives. Whether we are triathletes or couch potatoes, we're all running the race. But what are we running toward, exactly? Paul says to race toward an "imperishable" crown. We've traded in leafy crowns for gold medals for Olympic athletes, so the imagery Paul is using here can fly right over our heads. But the Bible promises specific imperishable crowns for those who surrender their lives to Christ. They are:

- The crown of rejoicing (1 Thess. 2:19)
- The crown of righteousness (2 Tim. 4:8)
- The crown of glory (1 Pet. 5:4)
- The crown of life (Rev. 2:10)

These are awards only God can give. He doesn't hand them out for perfect ballroom dances or mirrorball trophies. They are the awards given to those who live their lives for Him. Remember the qualifications for heroes given in Hebrews 11:1–2? "Now faith is the reality of what is hoped for, the proof of what is not seen. For our ancestors won God's approval by it."

The winners in God's kingdom are the runners who put their trust in Him. When we stop running aimlessly toward the prizes the world offers and start running headlong toward God, we exchange perishable prizes for the imperishable.

If the goal of marriage is to be happy, we will find that carrot constantly out of reach. Ultimately, our marriages can glorify God and paint a picture of the gospel. If we are trying to keep up with the Joneses, we will never satisfy our craving for more, but if the purpose of our lives and our stuff is to love like Jesus did, we will find that we have all that we need. If we just work for a paycheck, our job will be unsatisfying, but if we do all things for God's glory, we can persevere with grace and joy. See how that works? When we stop chasing after the things that cannot last, we are freed up to race toward things that are eternal.

I knew that God had chosen this opportunity for me. Along the way He exposed many perishable crowns that I had been racing toward: approval, perfection, applause. As He gently nudged me to lay them down, He offered an exchange. I could trade in approval addiction for the crown of glory He freely offered me. I could stop trying to be perfect and pick up the crown of righteousness. I could exchange fear of man for rejoicing. I could swap my will for His will and be given the crown of life.

A Grand Finale

I already felt like I'd won, but I still had to take my victory lap. I was shocked to find myself standing among the final three. The ride was almost over, but there was still work to be done. Immediately following the show on Monday, we were rushed back to the rehearsal studio to learn our final dance. We were allowed to practice from nine to midnight and our professional dancers choreographed new routines on the fly. We had three hours to learn a new dance and prepare to perform it during the live finale the following night.

Because of our extreme circumstances over the previous two days with Mark's injuries, my emotional and mental levels had hit their limit. I was too exhausted and tapped out to wrap my brain around learning a routine that very night so the producers allowed me to go home and get some sleep with the stipulation that I would be back at the rehearsal studio at 6:00 a.m. the following morning and would be deducted one hour of practice time, having two hours instead of three. I happily agreed, although Mark wasn't too thrilled. As always, he was a trooper and before I knew it, it was time for my final twirl around the *DWTS* stage.

As I waited for the show to start, I was absolutely overcome with emotion. It was mind-boggling for me to realize that something I had dreamed about for nine years had actually happened and was now coming to an end and what a ride it had been! It was beyond gratifying and yet there was also a big part of me that didn't actually want to win. My mom and my sister came to visit me in my dressing room right before the show and I burst into tears. I told them that I didn't want to come in first and asked them to pray with me that I would come in third.

In the weeks before the finale I had received thousands of comments on social media saying that I didn't deserve to make it this far. Whether I did or didn't, the words hurt, they made me feel guilty for beating out some of my other competitors we all knew were better dancers than me. I didn't want to face any more of that scrutiny. I knew that Meryl was the best dancer in the competition and that Amy was a close second with her truly inspiring story, and I wanted them to win because they were so deserving of the title. It wasn't a cop-out or a way of not feeling disappointed if I didn't win. Third place on *DWTS* truly was like winning the Stanley Cup, World Series, or the Super Bowl to me. I had far exceeded my own expectations and what I wanted to accomplish and would walk away feeling great no matter what. So after my samba fusion dance to Stevie Wonder's "Sir Duke" with a total combined score of 78 to Amy Purdy's 89 and Meryl Davis's 90, I was announced as the third place winner and was over the moon! I was so proud of myself for accomplishing all that I did. I think that the first-, second-, and third-place winners were chosen exactly as they should have been, and I was thrilled with how it turned out.

Fought the Good Fight

Immediately following the finale, the final four couples (James and Peta, Mark and me, Meryl and Maks, Amy and Derek), as well as four troupe dancers (Sasha, Artem, Lindsey, and Jenna), all hopped on a private jet and flew to New York City. We walked right off our plane and onto the set of *Good Morning America* followed by a series of other talk shows and follow-up press interviews. It was a whirlwind trip, one I'll never forget, especially with the group of people I'd come to know and love and who have become great friends. Amy, Mark, and I reminisced about our last night as we watched back the finale episode on my laptop together at our hotel. What a ride!

Soon enough I was back home in L.A. with my family. I traded in my dance costumes for my jeans and T-shirts, private jets for the carpool line.

Crossing the Finish Line

If we look at the Word, we see that Paul knew what it was like to be jostled between the ordinary and the extraordinary. In 2 Timothy, Paul is writing a letter to his friend and fellow missionary, Timothy. The context of the letter is that Paul was writing it from jail; this was his farewell letter to a friend he had experienced so much with.

In 2 Timothy 4:7 we find Paul using running to describe his faith once again. He says, "I have fought the good fight, I have finished the race, I have kept the faith."

I can almost see the relief on Paul's face as he wrote those words. The race was tough. It didn't come without hardship and heartache, but he had persevered. He could cross the finish line with his head high, because he never faltered in his faith.

I felt the same relief. I had done it! I fought the good fight. I finished the race. I kept the faith. My faith had carried me through deep valleys and steep peaks. As the roller coaster finally pulled into the station, God's faithfulness on the ride blew me away.

Yep, my *Dancing with the Stars* journey was over, but I still had a race to run. It was time to get back to the business of being a wife, mom, and actress. With renewed passion and courage to stand with conviction, I wanted to race to win the imperishable crowns in every area of my life.

Chapter 12

For Such a Time as This

*"If you keep silent at this time, liberation and
deliverance will come to the Jewish people from
another place, but you and your father's house will
be destroyed. Who knows, perhaps you have come
to your royal position for such a time as this."*
—Esther 4:14

A powerful man. A secret plot. A narcissistic mastermind. A beautiful woman. An elaborate beauty pageant.

Nope, these aren't the elements of the latest script I'm working on. These are the real-life details of Esther's life. Her story is told in just ten short chapters in the Old Testament book of Esther. If you've never read it, I hope you'll grab a Bible and do so now. Be prepared for action, adventure,

intrigue, romance, and plenty of plot twists! If you are familiar with Esther's story, I hope you'll take a moment and read
it again. There's gold in them thar hills!

Esther's story came to life for me several years ago
while studying Beth Moore's study *Esther: It's Tough Being
a Woman*. Since then, Esther has become one of my favorite books of the Bible and my hero. Did you know that the
name of God isn't even mentioned in the book of Esther? It's
true! Even so, the hand of God is an unmistakable theme in
Esther's story.

Let me take a moment to hit the highlights of Esther's
story. Trust me, you don't want to skim this!

Esther was a Jew. At the moment in history when Esther's
story is told, the Jews were in exile under the authority of foreign kings. Esther was an orphan, being raised by her cousin,
Mordecai. They lived in the Persian capital of Susa under the
rule of King Ahasuerus (also known as King Xerxes I).

The king threw a lavish party and tried to get his wife,
Queen Vashti, to parade in front of his drunk friends. Vashti
knew what it meant to stand with conviction, too, and
refused the king's request. The king's advisors told him that
if his own wife stood up to him in this way, wives across his
kingdom would soon defy their husbands. Something had to
be done! So Vashti was dethroned and banished. But this created another problem for the king. He had no queen.

Soon, an elaborate search for Vashti's replacement began.
Young, beautiful women from throughout the kingdom
were gathered and brought to the capital. There, they went
through twelve months of beauty treatments to make them
ready for the king. Talk about a spa day! Finally, each woman
was brought to the king so that he could pick his favorite.

The king loved Esther more than all the other women. She won more favor and approval from him than did any of the other young women. He placed the royal crown on her head and made her queen in place of Vashti. (Esther 2:17)

How did a young Jewish orphan become the queen to one of the most powerful men in the world? God arranged it! Scripture is clear that it was because of God's favor, not because of Esther's beauty, or wits, or riches that she was chosen as queen. God had an assignment for her that went well beyond picking out wedding china.

The king's advisor, Haman, had crafted an elaborate plan to annihilate the Jews, not knowing that Esther was one of them. He had successfully convinced the king to send out an edict that all of the Jews—men, women, and children—were to be killed on the same day and their belongings plundered. To be continued . . .

Judging by Esther's actions, I'd say that she and I have the same goal: to glorify God in everything we do. Esther knew what it was like to stand with conviction. She had an unwavering commitment to honor God and love His people. As a result, Esther left an incredible legacy. Thousands of years after Esther took a bold stand for God, the Jewish people still observe Purim, a traditional feast designed to celebrate what God does through dedicated and willing servants like Esther.

Esther is my hero! Talk about being willing to risk it all!

I may have danced and witnessed to twenty-five million viewers each week, but the entire Jewish population within 127 provinces stretching from India to Cush was in Esther's hands. If she was going to stand with conviction, the stakes would be sky high. In fact, in order to do what she knew was right, Esther had to risk her life. To go to the king without being summoned was an offense punishable by death. But Esther's cousin, Mordecai, urged her to take the risk.

The most known verse from Esther became significant to me as my life verse. This is Mordecai's desperate plea for Esther to stand up for what she believes despite the cost.

> If you keep silent at this time, liberation and deliverance will come to the Jewish people from another place, but you and your father's house will be destroyed. Who knows, perhaps you have come to your royal position for such a time as this. (Esther 4:14)

When I was doing Beth Moore's study on Esther, this particular verse popped off the page even though I had read it many times before. Suddenly I saw me in Esther's story. It was as if God was saying to me, *Candace, if you remain silent about Me in the entertainment industry, relief and deliverance for all people will arise from another place. My will will be accomplished, just through another source. But you and your father's family will perish. (Meaning you, Candace, and your legacy that I could leave through you and your family won't happen.) And who knows but that you, Candace, have come to a royal position* (Hollywood is kind of considered American royalty, isn't it?) *for such a time as this? You, Candace, right here, right now. The choice is yours.*

While Esther's story is certainly remarkable, it's not all that unique in some ways. At some point, we all come to a line in the sand where we make one of two choices. We will either stand with conviction, living out what we believe regardless of consequences, or we will bend to the whims of others and of culture, shaping and reshaping our beliefs in an attempt to fit in.

I know where I want to land. I want to be a woman of conviction! I want my beliefs formed through God's Word and His Spirit in me to be the rudder that steers my entire life rather than living aimlessly for the approval of the crowd.

Freshman Psychology

Lets take a quick detour to freshman-level Psychology for a minute. Today's lecture is on the Theory of Cognitive Dissonance. (Don't worry. There will not be a quiz and I promise it'll be quick!)

Cognitive Dissonance Theory states that we all have an inner drive to hold our attitudes and beliefs in harmony. We want what we believe to make sense and instinctively work to avoid disharmony (or dissonance).[16] If you're thinking, *Wait a minute! Can we get back to that juicy story about the beauty queen whose people were on the edge of destruction?* Don't worry, stick with me! Esther knew about cognitive dissonance, even if she didn't know to call it that.

We tend to look at the world around us and try to make what we see line up with what we already believe. Cognitive Dissonance Theory says that because of this, our *actions change what we believe* instead of allowing our *beliefs to change our actions.*[17]

But this is not how God calls us to live!

Ephesians 5:15 urges, "Pay careful attention, then, to how you walk—not as unwise people but as wise."

The wisdom of God that I have access to through His Word should change the way I live. I should move from someone who is unwise, thinking of things in a way that do not line up with God's Word to a woman of wisdom, thinking more and more like God does and learning to live more and more like He calls me to!

James 1:22 calls us to do more than just read the Bible. We are even supposed to do more than simply believe it. God asks us to let what we believe change how we live: "But be doers of the word and not hearers only."

Even though I still have so much to learn, I know what I believe.

- I believe God created me.
- I believe that God has a purpose for me.
- I believe that His Word is truth.
- I believe that God has called me to be salt and light in a dark world.

Those beliefs are true whether they feel like they are or not. They are true even when living them out is uncomfortable for me and others. I want those beliefs to shape how I live instead of letting how I live shape what I believe.

Esther must have had the same conviction. If you are on pins and needles waiting to hear the end of Esther's story, take a deep breath. Esther risked everything, including her own life, by approaching the king. She asked him to dinner, another bold move for a girl in Old Testament Persia! He agreed and on that high stakes date, Esther asked the king to spare her people. He did! Haman's wicked plot was exposed. He and his sons were hanged and the Jews were spared. For the icing on the cake, Esther's cousin, Mordecai, was given Haman's distinguished position in the kingdom. Because of Esther's bold move, many people throughout the kingdom of Persia turned their lives over to God.

In every province and every city, wherever the king's command and his law reached, joy and rejoicing took place among the Jews. There was a celebration and a holiday. And many of the ethnic groups of the land professed themselves to be Jews because fear of the Jews had overcome them. (Esther 8:17)

The Ripple Effect

When we stand with conviction, people will notice! This is the remarkable ripple effect of standing up for what we believe.

Since my time on *DWTS*, I am recognized more by fans when I'm out and about. I have a lot more people who follow my influence on social media, which I consider a huge part of my ministry. I've noticed that people really know me for my faith as well as my acting. (And that's really cool!) God chose a huge platform for Esther and then used His influence to accomplish His purposes. Many, many lives were impacted because Esther lived a life of courage and conviction. One of the cool things *DWTS* has done for me, is that it has given me an even larger platform to continue to encourage others in Jesus Christ. This isn't something new for me. I've done this regardless of the number of people I share with. When I decided to put my career on hold for ten years to be a full-time stay-at-home mom, my platform to share my faith with others wasn't any less important, it was just different. It may have been with a neighbor, the check-out gal at the grocery store, the person sitting next to me on an airplane or a new participant at church. Sharing my testimony and my faith in Jesus is a priority to me no matter how many people are listening. It's changed now in the fact that more people know me, know what I stand for, and know that I am a woman who wants to please the Lord.

After *DWTS*, I was in Vancouver shooting the first of several movies for the Hallmark Movies and Mysteries Channel in the Aurora Teagarden series. Typically each film has a new crew I work with that I'm not familiar with. I love getting to know new people and have an opportunity to make new friendships and work with talented people in their field. Does everyone know who I am, in the *Full House* sense? Mostly, yes, but not everyone, not always. But this time it felt a little different. Having just come off *DWTS*, I believe more people had a new perspective of me. I was reintroduced into their living room weekly on prime-time network TV, not that I'd gone anywhere . . . but if you don't have cable or watch all 500+ channels, you may have missed me.

With that said, the first day I walked on set was typical, introducing myself and meeting the crew I'd spend fourteen hours a day with for the next three weeks. On the second day, I noticed that when I walked into my trailer (which serves as my dressing room and resting place between scenes) the Christian band Third Day was playing on the radio. I immediately noticed and thought how cool that a Christian Top 40 song was on a pop radio station. Then the next song played and it was Chris Tomlin, another Christian singer. The Christian music just kept coming and I realized the station that was turned on was the local Christian station, which warmed my heart. I wondered if it was a fluke or if someone purposely set it there for me.

Later that morning, the head of the transportation department asked me, "Was the heat turned up and warm enough for you this morning in your room?" I said, "Yes, it was perfect! Thank you," and then I said, "Did you turn on the radio this morning too?" He said, "Yes, I did. I thought you'd like that station. It's my favorite one too," and gave me a little wink and a nod (code for: I'm a Christian too!). In all my years of working in entertainment, that was a first. My faith preceded me. He knew I was a Christian before I even got there and wasn't afraid to let me know he was too. I LOVED that!

Another instance while filming a movie soon after *DWTS*, I had a personal transportation driver from the crew that would take me to and from the set from my hotel. Sometimes the drive would be twenty minutes, sometimes an hour. I usually take the time to go over and memorize my lines for the day, make phone calls to Val and the kids, answer some e-mails, and read my Bible if I didn't wake up early enough to do it before I left. When I pull out my Bible, it's rare that someone doesn't ask me about it. I guess not as many people bring their Bible to work everyday in the entertainment industry as you'd think! LOL. If someone asks about it, I stop and know the door is open for conversation and I'm all over it! On one movie, I read the book of Esther aloud to my assistant/driver on the way to work most mornings and we talked through each chapter (after we had talked about faith and the Bible and if it was something she'd like to hear, which she openly said yes to).

On the other movie, my driver was very interested in knowing more about the Bible because his sister kept telling him he needed to read it. He thought it was a sign I was reading mine in the car. I told him it was! I told him God was after his heart, and I was just there to nudge him along to get to know the God who made him and loves him and wants him to know Him better. And then we had many wonderful conversations about God during our three weeks of driving an hour and back each day. No, they weren't all about God, but several were. I've found that being a "doer" of the Word and not just a "hearer" causes those kinds of conversations to happen a lot more often.

One particular morning, having just shared the gospel with someone, the camera operator, after a scene, said to me, "You have such a calmness about you today. I don't know what it is, but there's something so calming about your presence and a positive energy coming from you that is fantastic. I don't know what it is, but keep it up. It's nice to be around." I just giggled inside and praised God because I knew exactly what it was. God's favor was resting on me just like it did on Esther. The king might not have recognized what it was that drew him to Esther, but when she had the chance, she took the opportunity to share her beliefs with him. I knew that later, at the right time, I would share my source of strength and peace with that camera operator.

I know I talk about sharing my faith with others a lot because it's important to me and I really do it. The Bible tells us to go into the world and preach the gospel message, which is the greatest gift of love any of us will ever receive. I feel like when I don't prayerfully set my mind on doing that, I miss opportunities not only to plant a seed of faith into someone's life, but to grow mine as well. That's why before each movie I make, I pray for divine conversations on set and opportunities to share the gospel with others. And let me just say that this isn't the only thing I ever talk about. It probably only amounts to 10 percent of my conversations a day if that, but I purposefully seek to find a way to open that door if others are open to talking about it. I would never force this conversation on anyone if they weren't up for it.

Accepting Your Assignment

As I look back over my *DWTS* journey, I am so glad I decided to live with conviction instead of bending to the opinions of others. What if I had said "no" to this opportunity because some people worried I might compromise? I would have missed the chance to share my faith with millions of people. What if I hadn't been true to myself because I worried that I might step on some toes? Maybe the ride would have gone smoother. Maybe not. But I wouldn't be able to look back with pride, knowing that I had stuck to my convictions every step of the way. What if I decided that standing with conviction was simply too tough and chosen the easy path instead? I wouldn't be able to look my kids in the eye and encourage them to stand up for what they believe in the face of opposition, knowing that I hadn't finished the race.

The truth is, God calls all of us to live with conviction. In fact, He has given us each a very specific assignment. "Whatever you do, do it enthusiastically, as something done for the Lord and not for men" (Col. 3:23).

Whether you're a mama who spends her days kissing boo boos and dishing out Cheerios, or the CEO of a Fortune 500 company with a billion dollar budget to balance . . . whether you have a million Facebook friends, or none at all . . . whether you are young or old, rich or poor, an artist, an architect, a nurse, or a waitress, God has this assignment for you . . .

Do it *all* for Me. Live your life to honor Me, even when there is a cost.

If God can use a beauty pageant for a pagan king to save His people and draw many more to Him, He can use you. If He can use a reality show about dancing to tell His story to millions, He can use your life for big things if you will let Him.

One commentator wrote about Esther's story this way:

He used the beauty pageant. He used the playboy king. God's purposes touch the lives of the rich and poor, rulers and commoners, the godly and the wicked. There's nothing in this world outside the influence and sovereign purposes of God.

We also learn that each of us has an assignment. Esther's assignment of petitioning the king was risky and frightening. The outcome was uncertain. Mordecai emphasized that God would accomplish His purposes even if she refused to cooperate. But if God got someone else to do the job, she would lose the blessing, joy, and reward of faithful obedience. God provided Esther the strength and wisdom to do what He asked her to do, and the outcome was beyond what she could have imagined. Her story challenges us to look beyond our circumstances, limitations, and fears and ask the Lord, "What is your assignment for me?"[18]

As you read my story, that is the place that I want your heart to land. God has an assignment for you! He wants your life to be like salt, adding flavor to every situation. He wants you to look like a bright, shining city on a hill, something remarkably different from the ordinary landscape around you. He wants your story to point to a bigger story of His great love for each of us.

Sure, standing with conviction takes courage. You'll probably feel like you've been strapped into a roller-coaster ride with plenty of peaks and valleys! Sometimes you will want to scream with excitement. Other times, you may find your stomach is in your throat. But ultimately, if you do not stand for something, you will fall for anything.

I often think of the circumstances Esther faced. Life or death. Literally. And here I am, in the twenty-first century, not necessarily making life-or-death decisions, but decisions to honor God, my family, and my people that could ultimately cost me my job that I love. It really puts it in perspective. As much as I desire to make a living and support my family financially and appreciate greatly all that I have, speaking up for my values, my morals, and my God doesn't seem so difficult anymore compared to what Esther faced.

As you finish Esther's story, you will see that one choice to stand with conviction led to more choices to stand with conviction. She was emboldened to continue to fight for what was right and do all that she could to be a blessing to God's people. In the same way, my *DWTS* experience, though rocky at times, just increased my desire to live my life for God's glory. I want the same for you. My heart is stirred by imagining what could happen if each of you decided to do everything for God's glory and to let your beliefs change how you live. If you get to dance along the way, even better!

With that in mind, would you join me in asking this question?

God, what is Your assignment for me?

How to Find a Truth-Centered Church

If you're looking for a church that balances grace and truth, here are eight questions to consider.

Q. Does this church believe that the Bible is God's Word?

The Bible is the plumb line for truth!

John 17:17 says it plainly, "Your word is truth." Second Timothy 3:16 tells us that "all Scripture is breathed out by God" (ESV) and useful in teaching us how to be more like Him.

The Bible isn't just a good book. We can't throw it on a stack of other spiritual teachings and lump them together as "good" truths. Likewise, a church where teaching is heavy on personal antidotes and funny stories and light on biblical teaching isn't directing us toward the kind of truth that matters most. Look for a church that clearly believes that the Bible is the very Word of God and that it is where we should turn for answers.

Q. Does this church believe that Jesus is God's Son?

Does this church teach that Jesus is simply a good man or one of many spiritual teachers? If so, it's not the right place for you. When Jesus lived on the earth, many people tried to take the position that Jesus was just a teacher, or just a good guy, but Jesus corrected them. In fact, He was put on trial for those claims. Here's what you would have heard if you had been sitting in that courtroom (taken from Mark 14:61–62).

Judge: Are you the Messiah? Are you God's Son?

Jesus: I Am. One day you will see me sitting by God in heaven.

Jesus was sentenced to death because He refused to back down from His claim that He was God's Son who had come to rescue us through His death. If a church presents Jesus as something other than who He claimed to be, it's not a good fit.

Q. Does this church present the gospel?

Jesus said it Himself, "I am the way, the truth, and the life. No one comes to the Father except through Me" (John 14:6).

Distorting the gospel was a problem even in the earliest churches. Preachers would add to the message that Jesus' sacrifice was our only means of salvation. Maybe we need Jesus *and* good deeds to be saved? Maybe we need Jesus *and* to follow all the rules to be saved? But in Galatians 1:9, Paul blows the whistle and says, "No way! Don't stand for any other gospel than the one Jesus preached!" (my paraphrase).

Jesus' death on the cross paid the penalty for our sin. By believing in Him and surrendering our lives to Him, we are saved by grace alone and made right with God. Make sure that the church you attend preaches the one and only gospel. It is because of His grace, that we would choose to honor God and live a life pleasing to Him.

Q. Does this church care for the lost?

In Matthew 28:19–20, Jesus gives the first church leaders a two-part mission: "Go, therefore, and make disciples of all nations, baptizing them in the name of the Father and of the Son and of the Holy Spirit, teaching them to observe everything I have commanded you. And remember, I am with you always, to the end of the age."

Your church should be actively seeking to make disciples. That means reaching out to those who do not yet know Jesus. Pay close attention to how your church interacts with the community. Do they seek to love and care for those outside the church walls? What indicators are there that they are interested in the spiritual needs of those who don't know Christ?

Q. Does this church provide opportunities for me to grow?

The second part of the mission Jesus gave as part of the Great Commission was to train disciples. That means teaching the Bible to Christians.

Ask yourself:

- Are there opportunities at this church to grow in my knowledge of the Bible?

- Are there wise, older women here who can demonstrate mature faith?
- Are there opportunities for me to be stretched through service to others?
- Can I participate in training other disciples through this church by teaching Sunday school, leading a small group, etc.?

Q. Is Jesus the head of this church?

The Bible makes it clear that Jesus is the head of the church (Eph. 4:15). Every church will have human leadership that may include a pastor, elders, deacons, and administrators, but ultimately it should be obvious that the human leadership wants God to be in control.

Look for leadership that makes prayer a priority and has checks and balances through God's Word.

Q. Is repentance a dirty word here?

We all love feel-good sermons, the kind that send us off to Sunday lunch with warm fuzzies in our tummies. These might be sermons on God's love, or friendship, or the resurrection. There's nothing wrong with these sermons, but be wary if every message you hear at church is designed to make you feel good and avoids a regular call to repentance.

Jesus sure didn't shy away from repentance in any of His sermons. Matthew 4:17 tells us, "From then on Jesus began to preach, 'Repent, because the kingdom of heaven has come near!'"

James 5:16 commands us to confess our sins.

If the leadership of a church never teaches on sin, hell, and our need to repent, move on.

Q. Is this church "salt" and "light"?

In Matthew 5:13–14 Jesus was describing the believers who make up the church when He said, "You are the salt of the earth. . . . You are the light of the world. A city situated on a hill cannot be hidden."

As Christians, we should stick out because we let the Bible inform how we live instead of the culture. Look for a church that tries to influence the culture rather than being influenced by the culture.

Appendix B

Growing Your Faith

I'm often asked how my faith is so strong. It's because I spend time reading and studying the Bible. Without knowing the Bible for myself, I wouldn't know what was truthful or false. I also wouldn't have the faith I have today. If you don't know your Bible, you won't know God. I've been doing group Bible studies for many years. Some years I'd meet weekly with about seven women at my home, and other years I've met with larger women's groups at church. Spending time daily studying God's Word is essential, and following that up with a weekly group study is where I've always seen the most growth and understanding in myself. There is also built-in accountability by simply showing up and when we dig in, hear stories and testimonies from other women who have a deeper understanding of some of the Scriptures, or simply more life experience, it grows us beyond what we can just do alone. That's why community is so important and biblical.

My favorite studies have been the ones that have weekly DVDs to watch along with five days of homework in between. A few of my favorite Bible teachers who have these types of studies are Beth Moore, Priscilla Shirer, Kelly Minter, and Angela Thomas. Here are some specific studies I've grown from.

Esther: It's Tough Being a Woman by Beth Moore

This is the study that brought the book of Esther to life for me as I mentioned in chapter 12. I discovered my life verse while doing this study and was inspired to boldly stand for God's truth.

Daniel: Lives of Integrity, Words of Prophesy by Beth Moore

My all-time favorite study is *Daniel* by Beth Moore. I did it many years ago, but it's still a study I think about often and continues to prick at my heart when I make life and character decisions. Daniel's story is all about courage and conviction. Before I did this study, I only thought of the story of Daniel as a man who was spared in the lions' den because he honored God. My knowledge was basically at an elementary Sunday school level, until I did Beth's study. I had no idea what a brave man Daniel was, not just because he faced the lions and had faith, but because he didn't compromise his convictions from the first day he was brought into the chief official's presence after his city had been besieged. He and a few friends separated themselves from the others in such a way that the king took notice. He couldn't find anyone equal to Daniel in wisdom and understanding. Daniel lived a countercultural life and people noticed! He was elevated in position and yet never compromised himself as he climbed the corporate ladder and had his character attacked by those who were jealous. Daniel had the type of heart and conviction I want to emulate.

Gideon: Your Weakness. God's Strength by Priscilla Shirer

I learned a lot from Priscilla Shirer's study of Gideon last year, especially finding God's strength in my weakness. The first step to Gideon's greatness was that he was an open vessel, willing and eager to be used by God. I can relate! It's my life's mission to be that vessel and instrument of God even when I don't feel like I'm experienced enough, good enough, wise enough, or strong enough.

At the end of the study, my eyes were really opened and I could relate to Gideon more than I wished to. Gideon figured if God showed him favor in one area, He'd certainly continue to show favor no matter what Gideon decided to do, even if he never talked to God about it. Gideon was wrong.

Here's a brief overview of some of the notes I took at the end of the study. You'll notice they're not all complete sentences. I was just writing what I was thinking. At the time, I was struggling about whether or not to continue the speaking circuit at women's inspirational and Bible conferences at various churches all over the country and tours like Extraordinary Women that I've been doing for the past ten years. While it is a huge way to share the gospel and my testimony to others, I was simply getting burned out. I felt a pressure and guilt that I would be letting God down if I didn't continue because He gave me the platform in the first place. I asked myself if I was throwing away a God-given opportunity. I also would hear hundreds and thousands of women's stories who were blessed or related to mine when I spoke. That was an amazing feeling and sense of accomplishment for kingdom purposes. There was also a sense of financial security being on tours that was scary to give up. The time commitment to each event and scheduling up to two years in advance was also obligating me to pass on opportunities that I would have considered my first passions and dreams. And yet, I could never get around the fact that sharing the gospel is always a win-win situation. The study of Gideon was one of the instruments and confirmations I needed that helped me make my decision.

These are my own questions and answers to myself:

> **Question:** *What "logic" (in reality: lies) does the enemy use against me to disguise the spiritual nature of my struggles and mask his role in them?*

> **Me:** *(speaking Satan's lies in my head) God has failed you, Candace, in showing up for you at your speaking engagements when you've asked for specific requests to grow and challenge you in this area. He'll just do it again, so stop asking. Obviously He doesn't answer you, so just stop the speaking circuit.*

> **Lesson learned from Gideon:** *What if finishing well means not finishing? I realized I need to be aware of when my time is up. I never thought of this! Stopping doesn't always mean defeat. Could it be time to pass it on to someone else? Wait until another season in life? Philippians 3:13–14*

> *Mark 1:35–38—How did Jesus' communication with the Father keep Him on track?*

> *He stayed focused on His true task by being in constant communication with God. He stayed committed to His divine purpose for the Father, even if it meant disappointing the crowds. This was a big*

nudge to my soul. It would be okay to disappoint the crowds, if it wasn't what God intends for me at this time in my life.

I've been fitting His purpose into my life instead of pursuing His purpose. I have it backwards. It so easily gets twisted and off track. When was the last time I asked God, "Do You want me to continue speaking? I just assumed You did because it's for Your glory and I've been doing it for so long. Help me put down my own agenda and seek Yours. I know I do all things for You, God, but I don't always ask You if it's what You intended for me. I could be missing out on something else You have for me? I know You work for the good of those who love You, who have been called according to Your purpose. Romans 8:28

But changing some of these things scares the living daylights out of me! I don't want my dreams in other areas taken away from me. And yet, I don't have any reason to believe it will be or wouldn't be blessed by You as long as I pursue You in all of it. I know it's about being willing and open."

It's a relief to know that even if I don't finish triumphantly, God can and will still use me for His purpose for the sake of advancing His kingdom. That's not a cop-out for character or conviction; it's a pressure release and a weight I don't need to be carrying around.

I am a redemption story. My sin = His glory.

My redemption = His purpose, His plan, His glory.

Ultimately, I decided to stop speaking indefinitely and not commit to any future speaking events for a year, and then reevaluate at that time. And while it felt like a huge risk to stop the speaking circuit, God has opened many doors to my first passions in acting and entertainment, and 2014 proved to be an extremely successful year in many ways that could not have happened had I decided to continue booking speaking dates. *Dancing with the Stars* was one of them. I know there may be some skeptical people thinking a reality television show shouldn't come before sharing the gospel with others, and it didn't. God is still using me and allowing me to do it, simply in a different format that fits and fulfills who God inherently created me to be.

Notes

1. Candace Cameron Bure, *Balancing It All* (Nashville: B&H Publishing Group, 2014), 97.

2. Dannah Gresh, "Can Spirituality Impact a Woman's Sex Life?" *FOX News*, June 21, 2013, http://magazine.foxnews.com/love/can-spirituality-impact-womans-sex-life.

3. Roger Dooley, "Why Faking a Smile Is a Good Thing," *Forbes*, February 26, 2013, http://www.forbes.com/sites/rogerdooley/2013/02/26/fake-smile/.

4. Ibid.

5. Angela Thomas, "What the Bible Says about Joy," September 21, 2012, http://faithlifewomen.com/2012/09/what-the-bible-says-about-joy/.

6. Ibid.

7. Candace Cameron Bure, *Reshaping It All* (Nashville: B&H Publishing Group, 2011), 167.

8. "The 5 Points of Contact," accessed November 13, 2014, http://centurydancesport.com/ballroom-dance-dresses.

9. Kimberly Wagner, *Fierce Women* (Chicago: Moody Publishers, 2012), 20.

10. Ibid.

11. Susan August Brown, "Argentine Tango: A Brief History," accessed November 10, 2014, http://www.tejastango.com/tango_history.html.

12. "Mark Ballas Talks 'Dancing with the Stars' Finale," originally aired May 22, 2014, http://live.huffingtonpost.com/r/segment/dancing-with-the-stars-mark-ballas/537b7be502a76064c40006f0.

13. Karen Ehman, "What Candace Cameron Bure's Waltz Teaches Us about God," May 15, 2014, http://www.karenehman.com/2014/05/what-candace-cameron-bures-waltz-teaches-us-about-god.

14. "Australian Runner Cliff Young," accessed November 24, 2014, http://www.learning-disabilities-reading-tutor.com/australian-runner-Cliff-Young.html.

15. "Interview with Cliff Young," accessed November 24, 2014, http://www.coolrunning.com.au/ultra/1997032.shtml.

16. "Cognitive Dissonance," accessed November 24, 2014, http://changingminds.org/explanations/theories/cognitive_dissonance.htm.

17. Ibid.

18. ESV Women's Devotional Bible (Crossway, 2014), a devotional reading by Mary Kassian titled "Accepting Your Assignment" found on page 565.

Also Available from
CANDACE CAMERON BURE

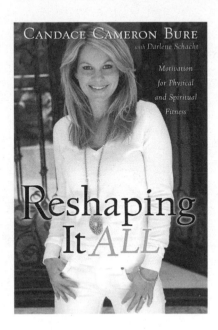

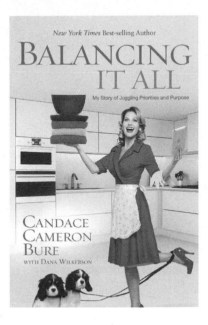

RESHAPING IT ALL
978-1-4336-6973-6

BALANCING IT ALL
978-1-4336-8184-4

Candace shares a candid account of her struggle with food and ultimately her healthy outlook on weight despite the toothpick-thin expectations of Hollywood. More than a testimony, here is a motivational tool that will put readers on the right track and keep them there. In addition to practical advice, Candace offers a biblical perspective on appetite and self control that provides encouragement to women, guiding them toward freedom.

"How do you do it all?" That's the question that wife, mom, actress, and best-selling author Candace Cameron Bure is often asked. And it's a question that women everywhere are asking themselves as we seek to balance all of our roles, responsibilities, and opportunities. Come along and dig into Candace's story from her start in commercials, the balance-necessitating years on Full House, to adding on the roles of wife and mom while also returning to Hollywood. Insightful, funny, and poignant, Candace's story will help you balance it all.